Python Machine Learning

A Practical Beginner's Guide for Understanding Machine Learning, Deep Learning and Neural Networks with Python, Scikit-Learn, Tensorflow and Keras

Brandon Railey

Copyright 2019 © Brandon Railey

All rights reserved.

No part of this guide may be reproduced in any form without permission in writing from the publisher except in the case of review.

Legal & Disclaimer

The following document is reproduced below with the goal of providing information that is as accurate and reliable as possible.

This declaration is deemed fair and valid by both the American Bar Association and the Committee of Publishers Association and is legally binding throughout the United States.

Furthermore, the transmission, duplication or reproduction of any of the following work including specific information will be considered an illegal act irrespective of if it is done electronically or in print. This extends to creating a secondary or tertiary copy of the work or a recorded copy and is only allowed with an express written consent from the Publisher. All additional right reserved.

The information in the following pages is broadly considered to be a truthful and accurate account of facts, and as such any inattention, use or misuse of the information in question by the reader will render any resulting actions solely under their purview. There are no scenarios in which the publisher or the original author of this work can be in any fashion deemed liable for any hardship or damages that may befall them after undertaking information described herein.

Additionally, the information in the following pages is intended only for informational purposes and should thus be thought of as universal. As befitting its nature, it is presented without assurance regarding its prolonged validity or interim quality. Trademarks that are mentioned are done without written consent and can in no way be considered an endorsement from the trademark holder.

Table of Contents

Introduction

Machine learning has transformed the way a business and organization operates. It is important for every business to understand patterns and trends in complex data to succeed or maximize profits. This understanding is becoming a key attribute that a company must use to grow in a challenging environment. You can use Python, and the many underlying libraries and directories to derive some key insights about the data you have. The unique capabilities of the language make it easier for you to build some sophisticated algorithms and models that will allow you to stem some insights about the data set.

From a business standpoint, machine learning can be used to understand how a customer thinks and behaves. Businesses can also use machine learning to predict the future profits or losses that the company may face. They can also use it to see when they should stock a specific product or when they should release a new product. Let us look at how a retailer can improve his or her sales through machine learning. The retailer can see when his or her customers purchase a specific product, and increase the stock for that product during that season. Walmart had realized that its customers wanted to purchase strawberries during a specific season, and the retailer increased the stock of strawberries in the store. This helped them improve on their profits. The same can be said about e-commerce websites as well.

Machine learning, cognitive computing and artificial intelligence are some terms that most people read about when it comes to advanced analytics. These subjects give a company an edge or an advantage over other businesses in the same industry. Every business leader is now facing an unanticipated and new competitor, and these leaders are looking for ways to develop new strategies that will help them prepare their business for the future. Businesses can always try a variety of strategies, but they all will boil down to one fact – you must always follow the data. This book will help you learn more about how you can use machine learning to delve into the data, and how you can derive some predictions from that data. You will also learn what you should think about when it comes to machine learning, and also see what how you can analyze data using different machine learning algorithms.

Machine learning is a topic that is discussed in almost every organization in any industry. Most organizations choose to use machine learning algorithms to identify new ways to make use of the data that they collect. So, why should you add machine learning to your processes? If you use the right machine learning algorithms, you can predict how a business or how a customer will act. You can always predict what will happen next. When you constantly add new data to the algorithm or model, the machine will learn from that data and update the solution as often as it can. The value of doing this is evident – if you use the correct data in a machine learning model and constantly update that data, you can predict the future with ease.

Machine learning is a subset of artificial intelligence, and this method of learning allows any machine to gather information from input data. This means that we will not be using any explicit commands or code to explain to the system about what it will need to do. That being said, it is not easy to implement machine learning models in a business. A machine learning will use different algorithms that learn only from the data, and derive methods that can be used to improve, describe or predict the outcomes. When the machine takes in more data, you can ensure that you train the machine well to produce accurate results.

Once you train the model, and give it some new data, it should provide you with an output. For instance, if you use a predictive algorithm, you will create a predictive model. When you feed that model with any new data, the machine will give you an output that is based on the training data set that you had initially used. Machine learning is now being used extensively to develop some analytics model.

You may have interacted with many machine learning applications in the past. For instance, if you visit Amazon or Flipkart and begin to view products, you will be presented with other products that are similar to what you were looking at. These recommendations are not coded into the system, but are suggestions that are given to you through a machine learning model. The model will look at all your history and use that information to present you with similar products.

There are different types of machine learning algorithms that a business can use depending on the type of information or data it has available. For example, if the business has a labeled data set, it can use any supervised machine learning algorithm to predict the future. On the other hand, if the business did not have a labeled data set, it could use some unsupervised machine learning algorithm to train the model to derive an output. This book covers some of the most commonly used machine learning algorithms.

Throughout this book, you will gather information on what machine learning is, and how you can build your very own model in Python using SciKit learn. If you want to learn more about machine learning, deep learning and neural networks, and how you can build these models in Python, this book is invaluable. This book covers the use of the NumPy and Pandas libraries in Python and will help you build a machine learning model and a neural network in SciKit-learn using those libraries. You will come across some examples of code that will help you understand the steps you will need to follow when it comes to building a machine learning application or a neural network. It is only when you understand these codes fully that you should start with building your applications.

I hope this book will help you gather more insights on what machine learning is, and how you can use it to analyze different data sets.

Chapter One:
An Introduction to Machine Learning

Machine learning is a process through which machines with inbuilt artificial intelligence or AI often learn processes, probability, identifying problems and solutions. Such machines are used for data analysis, recognition, predictions, diagnosis and projections. They learn from training data, a sample database that is identical to the entire population, to identify different patterns within the data and to use those patterns, as well as help find solutions to problems. Out of the various methods of learning mechanisms used to help a machine learn, unsupervised machine learning, reinforcement learning and supervised machine learning are the most common amongst them. The following chapters will cover these concepts.

In a layman's language, the change in the

structure of a machine to enhance its performance is a classic example of how a machine learns.

Let's say if a machine must predict which team will win the Barclays Premier League. The programmer will train or feed the machine with historical data about the team's performance and the player's performances. Using such information and data the machine can identify a pattern and correlations between the data points or variable in the data set. The machine can then use these patterns and predict which team will win the Barclays Premier League.

Skeptics often wonder why machines must learn since they are pretty aware of what these machines are capable of. Facebook has used machine learning and AI to develop a machine trained with specific vocabulary dataset. It's scary how this machine used the alphabets that are found in the data to create its own language, a language humans find difficult to understand. If multiple machines learn this language, then they can communicate amongst themselves. Regardless of the outcome, Google and Facebook are training machines to learn through continuous feeding of datasets.

There are many reasons as to why machine learning is important. Psychologist are using some of these concepts of machine learning to help understand and better evaluate human beings and their mind.

Subjects Involved in Machine Learning

Machine learning uses concepts from various subjects. The field of machine learning is developing as you read this book and hence the subjects mentioned are not an exhaustive list. However, the subjects mentioned below along with the concepts are the foundation of machine learning.

Statistics

Regression, clustering, data analysis and hypothesis testing are few of the concepts in statistics that are the foundation of machine learning. Most machine learning algorithms use these concepts to train machine which is a common problem in both statistics and machine learning. Training is the process where various sample datasets help machine pull out information about the population. The Machines store this information and use it to predict or project futuristic outcomes and values. The machine can also identify a problem and its solution to that particular problem using the training dataset. Another problem that is common to both statistics and machine learning is the identification of the values of a function at a given point. Solutions to such problems are the instances that the machine uses to evaluate the estimation of future events that often use data from the past.

Brain Modeling

Neural networks in the brain are often referred to as a concept that is closely related to machine learning. Scientists have a theory that one can replicate the model of the neurons in the human brain and build a nonlinear neural network. This layer in this network has nodes, and the engineer can assign a weight of values to those nodes to calculate the output. Psychologist and scientist are now using neural networks to understand human learning better with exploring few spheres being symbolic processing, connectionism and brain style computation to understand human and machine learning better.

Adaptive Control Theory

When a system controls the efficiency to an adaptive change in their system has been theorized as Control theory. The environment change has been the root cause of many issues a system faces during a change. The idea is to make the system capable enough to anticipate any changes in the environment to adapt and maintain the efficiency and accuracy of the machine.

Evolutionary Models

Evolutionary theories conclude that human beings and animals both learn not only to adapt to a certain environmental change but also to learn, evolve and perform better. The concept of learning and evolution that revolves around human learning is the same from machine learning as well. The methods that psychologists use to understand human learning would intern help scientists improve how a machine learns and evolves.

Varieties of Machine Learning

So far this book has introduced you to what machine learning is all about and answered the question about the subjects that constitute it. Now we come to the more important question of what can be learned about machine learning. Following are a few topics on which insights and knowledge can be gained through understanding machine learning:

- Programs and Logic rule

- Terminology and grammar

- Finite state machines

- Problem - Solving systems

- Functions

- AI or Artificial intelligence

- Statistics

Of the above, the two most important topics are

those of statistics and artificial intelligence. These two subjects are extensively used in machine learning. Now we'll move on to chapters that describe two broad categories in machine learning techniques: supervised machine learning and unsupervised machine learning.

Uses of Machine Learning

Most organizations and large Enterprises used machines to complete manual tasks that were once impossible by humans to complete within a short period, especially when large volumes of data were involved. In the last few decades, the availability of data has rapidly increased making it impossible for human beings to analyze it. This increase in the volume of data has paved the way for automated processes in machines to work on tasks that are difficult for human beings to accomplish or complete. In other words, machine learning is helping in reducing the man-hours drastically.

We have stepped into the world of business analytics, big data, data science and artificial intelligence, that help derive useful information from data analysis that can help us drive our businesses and lives for the better.

Predictive analysis is no more a piece of cake for the large Enterprises but also for the small businesses that have a chance to participate in the process of collecting and utilizing information effectively.

Let us now learn some technical use machine learning that can be applied to the real world problems. Data Replication

Machine learning allows the model or its algorithm to develop data that looks like the training dataset. For example, if you run a manuscript through the machine, it identifies the density of the words on every page of the manuscript. The output is a text that is identical to the words or data present in the manuscript.

Clustering Variables

Clustering algorithms are used to group variables that may be related to one another, which will be covered in a later chapter. This is useful when you are not sure of how changes made to one variable affect the machine and the outcome along with other variables in the group. When datasets are huge, the machine looks for latent variables and uses them to learn more about acquired data.

Reduction of Dimensionality

Since data always has variables and dimensions, it is tough for human beings to gather some understanding from data that has more than three dimensions. Machine learning reduces these dimensions of the data to understand better by clustering similar or identical variables together. This process helps human beings to understand and identify functions within and between these variable clusters.

Visualization

There have been situations when a user wants a visually represented relationship between variables or to obtain a summary of the data. Machine learning helps in these processes by summarizing the data using specified or non-specified parameters.

Advantages and Disadvantages of Machine Learning

Some disadvantages of machine learning are:

- You always train the model using a training data set and then use a new data set to validate the model.

- This test data set is new to the model, which makes it difficult for you to identify any bias that exists within the model.

- When you cannot identify the bias, you cannot be certain that your inferences are correct.

- Some social scientists will only rely on these machine learning models. They forget that improvements have to be made when it comes to unsupervised machine learning models.

Some advantages of machine learning are:

- Human beings can never process large volumes of data, which makes it difficult to analyze that data.

- Real-time data is produced in large volumes, and an automatic system will help you understand and analyze that data.

Applications of Machine Learning

Healthcare

Practitioners and doctors can now predict with high accuracy how long a patient who is suffering from a terminal illness will survive. Many medical systems are designed to learn from the training data set. These machines will help a patient avoid undergoing unnecessary tests. A radiologist's work is now obsolete because of machine learning. It is believed that machine learning when used to make medical decisions, can save up to $100 billion which could then be used to create novel tools for insurers, patients and doctors. It is true that a robot or a machine cannot replace a nurse or doctor, but technology will transform the healthcare industry.

Drug Manufacturing and Discovery

It takes time to discover and manufacture any new drug, and this process is very expensive. The company will need to test thousands of compounds to verify if the drug they have developed is indeed good for use. Of the many issues with testing drugs, the one that poses a huge difficulty is that only one combination can be used as a drug. Some machine learning algorithms can be used to improve this process.

Personalized Medication or Treatment

When you have an ache in your stomach or your head, you walk into your doctor's office and tell him your symptoms. Your doctor inputs those symptoms into the computer and narrows down on a probable cause. The system may also provide the doctor with the latest research on what he needs to know about the problem. He may ask you to take an MRI, and the computer will help the radiologist identify the problem if it is too hard for the human eye to identify. In the end, the computer will use your health records and your family medical history, compare it to the latest results and advice a treatment for you. Machine learning helps to make treatment and medication more personal.

Personalized treatment will grow in the future, and machine learning will play a vital role in finding what genes or genetic markers are responsible for the diseases and which ones will respond to the treatment.

Finance

Over 90% of the top financial institutions and organizations in the world use machine learning and advanced data analytics. Through machine learning, banks have developed the ability to offer personalized services to customers with better compliance and lower costs. They are also able to generate higher revenue.

Machine learning also helps to detect fraud. Let us assume that you are at home and watching an episode of Game of Thrones when you get a call from your personal banker asking you if you have made a purchase of $Y in a store near your home. However, you did not make that purchase using your card, and the card is in your wallet. So, why did the bank flag this purchase alone? Machine learning has to do with this.

The finance and banking sectors use machine learning to combat fraud. It is best to use machine learning since it can scan through large volumes of transactional data, and detect or identify any unusual behavior. A transaction made by a customer is often analyzed in real-time, and a score is given to that transaction to represent how fraudulent it may be. If the score is above a threshold, the machine will flag the transaction.

Retail

The Realities of Online Personalization Report stated that close to 45% of retailers are using machine learning to provide their customers with product recommendations that are based on the user's shopping history. Every customer looks for a personal shopping experience, and the recommendations always increase the conversion rates thereby increasing the revenue for retailers.

Statistical Arbitrage

Statistical Arbitrage, a term that is used often in finance, refers to trading strategies that are used by individuals in the industry to identify the short-term securities that can be invested in. In these strategies, the user always tries to implement an algorithm on an array of securities that are based on the general economic variables and historical correlation of the data. The measurements are cast as estimation or classification problems. The basic assumption made is that the price will always move towards a historical average.

Machine learning methods are applied to obtain a strategy called the index arbitrage. Linear regression and support vector regression is used at different prices of a fund and on a stream of stocks. The next step is to reduce the number of dimensions in the data set, and this is done using the Principal Component Analysis. In this analysis, trading signals are identified by modeling the residuals. This process is termed as a mean reverting process.

In this study, the different categories can be sold, buy, hold, do nothing for each security. You can then predict the expected return for a security over a future period. The estimates are often used to decide on whether the investor should buy or sell securities.

Prediction

Every bank will need to calculate the probability that there will be at least one applicant who will default on the repayment of a loan. If you want to calculate this probability, you will need to develop a system that will identify, clean and classify the data into different clusters or categories. This is performed based on some criteria that an analyst sets out. When the classification is complete, the system can calculate the probability. These calculations are made across different departments for different purposes.

Prediction is a machine learning algorithm that has gained immense popularity over the last few years. Most retailers only have reported on the sales they have made over the last ten or twenty years. This information is called historical information, and the process of reporting it is called historical reporting. You can use this information to predict what future sales will be like for the company. This information can help the business make the right decisions.

Steps in Building a Machine Learning System

Some common steps must be followed when building a machine learning model, regardless of the type of algorithm you want to use.

Define Objective

The first step is to identify the objective and define it well. This objective should explain the purpose behind the model. The type of algorithm you will use, the data you will need to source, and some other factors depend on the objective. You will also need the objective to help any other user understand what predictions can be made using the model.

Collect Data

This is one task that takes time to perform when you build a machine learning model. You can collect all the relevant information that you need to obtain to train the machine.

Prepare Data

This step is often overlooked by users and engineers. This will lead to many mistakes in the database. It is always good to clean the data and ensure that it is relevant to your objective. This will improve the predictions.

Select Algorithm

You can choose different types of algorithms like regression, classification, support vector machines, Naïve-Bayes, etc. The algorithm you choose is dependent on the objective that you have chosen.

Train Model

When you have the data ready, you should feed

the model with the data, and train the algorithm to perfection.

Test Model

Once your model is trained, it is now ready to start reading the input to generate appropriate outputs.

Predict

You can perform multiple iterations to ensure that the model predicts the results with high accuracy.

Deploy

When you test the model and are happy with the way it works, you can integrate that model into an application where you think it should be used. It is at this stage that you know that the model can be deployed.

The order of these steps will vary depending on the type of application you are developing, and whether or not you are using a supervised or unsupervised machine learning algorithm.

Chapter Two: Facts about Machine Learning

Machine learning is permeating numerous aspects of our everyday lives, right from optimizing Netflix recommendations to Google searches. Machine learning has contributed to improving different facets of building mechanics in smart building and to also improve the experiences of the occupants. You do not have to have a Ph.D. to understand the different facets and functions of machine learning. This section covers some facts about machine learning which are very basic and important to know.

Bifurcation of Machine Learning

Supervised and unsupervised machine learning are two techniques that programmers and scientists use to help machines learn. Smart buildings incorporate both types. Here is a simple example of how these types of machine learning look like: Let us assume that you want to teach a computer to recognize an ant. When you use a supervised approach, you will tell the computer that an ant is an insect that could either be small or big. You must tell the computer that the ant could either be red or black. When you use an unsupervised approach, you will need to show the computer different animal groups and then tell the computer what an ant looks like and then show the computer another set of pictures and ask the computer to classify the image as an ant until the computer learns the features specific to an ant.

Smart building spaces use both supervised and unsupervised machine learning techniques. The applications in these smart buildings allow the users to provide feedback to the building to improve the efficiency of the building.

Machines are not Fully Automatic

Machine learning helps computers automate, anticipate and evolve but that does not mean that they can take over the world. Machine learning uses algorithms that human beings develop. Therefore, machine learning still needs human beings since they will need to set parameters and train the machine with different training datasets.

Machine learning helps a computer discover patterns that are not possible for human beings to see. The computer will then adjust the system. It is, however, not good to identify and understand why those patterns exist. For instance, smart buildings. Human beings created smart buildings to improve the living conditions and the experiences that people have. One cannot expect that a machine will learn to become more productive. A human must set up the definitions and rules that the building will need to follow.

It is important to remember data cannot always

explain why any anomalies or outliers occur. Consider a scenario where the people in the building constantly request that the temperature of the building must reduce by 20 degrees when compared to the external environment. The machine learning algorithm will take this request into account, and notify the operator about the request. Therefore, it is essential that people operate the machines and verify that the conclusions that are derived are accurate.

Anyone can use Machine Learning

Writing a machine learning algorithm is very different from learning how to use that algorithm. After all, you do not need to learn how to program when you use an app on your phone. The best platforms always create an abstract of the program to present the users with an interface which need minimal training to use. If you do know the basics of machine learning, and some of the algorithms you are ready to go! Data scientists must edit or change the algorithms.

Machine learning has come of this age and is growing quickly. Buildings now use machine learning in different ways to make the existing infrastructure efficient and help to improve the experience of the occupants residing in the building. Right from an energy usage standpoint, buildings are always learning and analyzing the needs of the occupants.

How does this affect us going forward? This development in machine learning has made the world understand that anything can happen in the world without us asking. Machine learning engineering could go beyond managing lighting and temperature. Machine learning implies that there will be some future state of multiple layers and levels of automation that will need to be adjusted on the basis of current activity.

Data Transformation is Where the Work Lies

When you read through the different techniques of machine learning, you will probably assume that machine learning is mostly about selecting the right algorithm and tuning that algorithm to function accurately. The reality is prosaic – a large chunk of your time goes into cleansing the data and then transforming that data into raw features that will define the relationship between your data.

Revolution of Machine Learning has Begun

During the 1980s there was rapid development and advancement in the calculations that a computer can make. This led to some objections being raised against artificial intelligence, computers and machine learning which could help the world solve numerous ailments – right from household drudgery to diseases. As the fields of machine learning and artificial intelligence developed as formal fields of study, turning these ideas and hopes into reality was harder achieve, and artificial intelligence retreated into the world of theory and fantasy. However, in the last decade, the advances in the storage of data and computing have changed the game again. Machines are now able to work on tasks that once were difficult for them to learn.

Machine Learning is a Subset of Artificial intelligence

It is important for you to understand that machine learning is a process that drives data mining, and it is a subset of artificial intelligence. What is the difference between these terms? Experts spend hours debating on where they must draw the line between machine learning and artificial intelligence.

Artificial intelligence allows machines to think

like human beings. At any given minute, human beings can capture thousands of data points using the five different senses. The brain can recall memories from the past, draw conclusions based on causes and effects and make decisions. Human beings learn to recognize patterns, but every being has a limit.

One can think of machine learning as a continuous and automated version of data mining. Machines use data mining to detect certain patterns in data sets that human beings cannot find. Machine learning is a process that can reduce the size and volume of the data set. This will help the machine detect and extrapolate patterns that will allow us to apply that information to identify new actions and solutions.

In smart building spaces, machine learning enables any building to run efficiently while also responding to occupants' changing needs. For instance, you can look at how a machine learning application can do more when compared to how a smart building may handle a recurring board meeting. However, any machine learning algorithm can make sense of more than a thousand variables at any given time of the year to create an ideal thermal environment during the business meeting.

Chapter Three: Types of Machine Learning

Supervised Machine Learning

Supervised machine learning uses training datasets to help machines learn. These datasets contain various examples that consist of the input and the desired output, commonly known as supervisory signals. Machines use supervisory learning algorithms that help to generate inferred functions that forecast or predict events. These functions are called classifiers if the output is discrete and regression functions if the outputs are continuous. The supervisory algorithm must conceive a generalized method that helps the machine reach the desired output. Human beings and animals learn in a similar way through concepts. For example, if you are in a trigonometry class, you will learn many functions that you should use to solve specific problems. Let us look at how the supervised machine algorithm works.

Step 1

The engineer must determine what types of example should be a part of the training dataset. The engineer must be careful with the training dataset since the machine learns from the examples in the set. He must ensure that the examples have the right input and output. For example, if the machine must learn to recognize speech, the engineer must provide examples of words, sentences, paragraphs or phonemes. If the engineer provides the machine with numbers or images, the machine is not going to produce the desired output.

Step 2

The engineer must collect the data and clean it before she uses it as the training dataset. The dataset must represent all the possible outcomes and functions that the machine can develop for some input. The engineer must ensure that she maps the input examples with their correct outputs.

Step 3

The engineer must now decide how the input examples she should provide to the machine. This step is important since the accuracy of the machine is solely dependent on the representation of the input. Vectors represent the data, and this vector contains information about the attributes and characteristics of the variables in the data set. For example, if the store has the information about the products using one of the inputs, the input vector can contain the following:

- Product Name
- Brand
- Product Type

- Manufacturer

- Distributor and so on.

However, the machine must learn only to include some attributes to avoid a long training period. Many features may also lead to failure since the machine cannot identify or predict the output.

Step 4

The engineer must decide on what the structure of that function should be such that the machine can use it easily. She must also identify the algorithm that the machine should use to obtain the desired output. Common algorithms used are regression, clustering and decision trees.

Step 5

The engineer must then complete the design. She should run the algorithm on the dataset. There are some control parameters that the engineer must enter so that the algorithm works well. Cross-validation methods help to estimate the parameters. If the dataset is large, it is best to break the set into smaller subsets and use the cross-validation method to estimate the parameters.

Step 6

Once the algorithms run and the machine generates the function, the engineer should measure the accuracy of the function. The engineer must use a testing dataset instead of the training dataset to check the accuracy of the function.

There are many supervised machine learning algorithms in use, and each of these algorithms have their respective advantages and disadvantages. The selection of the learning algorithm is an essential step in the process since the engineer cannot use a definitive algorithm to train the machine.

Issues to Consider in Supervised Learning

With the usage of supervised learning algorithms, there arise a few issues associated with it. Given below are four major issues:

Bias-variance Tradeoff

The bias-variance tradeoff is an issue that every engineer should be wary of while working with machine learning. Consider a situation where we have various but equally good training sets. If the engineer uses multiple data sets to train the system, the algorithm will form a bias towards the input. Machines often give systematically incorrect outputs if the machine forms a bias to the input. Learning algorithms have a high input variance, which occurs when the algorithm causes the machine to predict different outputs for that input in each training set. The prediction error for the classifier function is calculated as the sum of the variance and the bias of the learning algorithm. There exists a tradeoff between the variance and the bias. One of the requirements of the learning algorithm is that it needs to have a low bias. This will ensure that the algorithm is flexible enough to accommodate all the data sets. However, if they are too flexible, the learning algorithms might end up giving varying outputs for each training set and hence increase the variance. A supervised machine learning algorithm should always find a way to adjust the tradeoff which happens automatically. The alternative is to use an adjustable parameter.

Function Complexity and Amount of Training Data

This issue with a supervised learning algorithm is concerned with the training data. The training dataset must be prepared depending on what time of function the machine should generate, a classifier or a regressor. If the function must be simple, a simple learning algorithm that has a low variance and high bias, can help the machine learn.

However, on many occasions, the function will be complex if there are many input variables or factors. The machine must act differently for different parts of the input vector. In such cases, the machine can only learn through a large training dataset. These cases also require the algorithms used to be flexible with low bias and high variance. Therefore, efficient learning algorithms automatically arrive at a tradeoff for the bias and variance depending on the complexity of the function and the amount of training data required.

Dimensionality of the Input Space

Dimensionality of the vector space is another issue that the engineer must deal with. If the input vector includes many features, the learning problem will become difficult even if the function only considers a few of these features as valuable inputs. Since there are many input variables, the input vector will have many dimensions which can lead to confusion. This situation ultimately leads to the first issue that we discussed. So, when the input dimensions are large, the engineer should adjust the value of the classifier to offset the effects of a high bias and low variance. The engineer could manually remove the irrelevant features and improve the efficiency and accuracy of the machine learning algorithm. This might not always be a practical solution. In recent times, some algorithms can remove unnecessary features and retaining only the relevant ones. This concept, called dimensionality reduction, will help you map the input data to fewer dimensions thereby improving the performance of the algorithm.

Noise in the Output Values

The final issue on this list is concerned with the interference of some noise, also known as an error, in the output value. These values will be wrong in some situations since there is some noise associated with the sensors. There is a chance that these values are wrong since there is an error in the code. In these cases, the learning algorithm will map the input variables to a specific output variable using the training data set. For such cases, algorithms with high bias and low variance are desirable.

Other Factors to Consider

The engineer must always consider the heterogeneity of data. She must choose an algorithm that considers the level of heterogeneity of the data. Some algorithms work better on datasets with a limit on the number of inputs used. Some examples are support vector machines, logistic regression, neural networks, linear regression and nearest neighbor methods. Nearest neighbor and support vector machines methods with Gaussian kernels work especially better with inputs limited to small ranges. On the other hand, there exist algorithms like decision trees which work very well with heterogeneous data sets.

There is a possibility that the dataset is redundant. A few algorithms perform poorly in the presence of high redundancy. This happens due to numerical instabilities. Examples of these types of algorithms are logistic regression, linear regression and distance-based methods. The engineer must include regularization to ensure that the algorithm performs better.

While choosing algorithms, engineers need to consider the amount of non - linearities in the inputs and the interactions within different features of the input vector. If there is little to no interaction and each feature contributes independently to the output, algorithms based on distance functions and linear functions perform very efficiently. However, when there are some interactions within the input features, it is best to use the decision trees and neural network algorithms. These algorithms detect the interactions between the input vectors. If the engineer decides to use linear algorithms, he must specify the interactions that exist.

The engineer can compare various algorithms before she chooses the one to address a specific application. However, she must spend some time and collect training data and tune the algorithm to ensure it works for the application. If provided with many resources, it is advisable to spend more time collecting data than spending time on tuning the algorithm because the latter is extremely tedious. The most commonly used learning algorithms are neural networks, nearest neighbor algorithms, linear and logistic regressions, support vector machines and decision trees.

Unsupervised Machine Learning

Unlike supervised machine learning algorithms, these algorithms infer or predict the outcomes from a data set that has no labels. You cannot apply an unsupervised learning method to a classification or regression problem since you are unaware of what the output data should be. This will make it impossible to train the machine in the usual way. You can use these algorithms to uncover the underlying structure and relationships in the data set.

Why is Unsupervised Machine Learning Important?

Through supervised machine learning algorithms, you can derive approximations of the results. Unsupervised machine learning algorithms can be used to uncover some underlying relationships or patterns within the data set which were previously unknown. Since you are unaware of what the outcomes should be, it is hard to determine if the results are accurate. This makes it easier to apply any supervised machine learning algorithm to a real-world problem.

You should use unsupervised machine learning algorithms when you have insufficient data about the required results. For example, you can use an unsupervised machine learning algorithm to identify the market you should target to launch a new product. If you are, however, trying to understand your customer base, you should stick to supervised machine learning algorithms.

Some applications of unsupervised machine learning algorithms include:

1. Through clustering, you can split the variables into different data sets on the basis of their similarity. Cluster analysis, however, tends to overestimate the similarities between the different variables and stops treating the variables as distinct data points. It is for this reason why most people do not choose cluster analysis in applications that look at customer segmentation.

2. Through anomaly detection, you can identify any irregularities in the data set. This will help you identify any fraudulent transactions, identify some outliers caused

due to human error or identifying some faulty pieces of some tools or hardware.

3. Through association mining, you can identify the groups of items that frequently occur in the data set. Most retailers use this approach for basket analysis since it allows them to identify the goods that are purchased by a group of customers at the same time. This will help them develop effective branding and marketing strategies.

4. If you want to reduce the number of features in any data set (dimensionality reduction) or want to break the data set into multiple components, you can use some latent variable models.

5. You can use the information that you obtain from any unsupervised machine learning algorithms when you implement a supervised machine learning algorithm. For instance, you can use an unsupervised

machine learning algorithm to identify the clusters in the data set. You can use these clusters as an additional feature in a supervised machine learning algorithm.

Reinforcement Learning

Another branch of machine learning is called reinforcement learning. This type of learning is all about taking the right action in any situation to maximize the reward. Many machines and software use this learning to identify the best path or behavior that the machine should use in a specific scenario. Reinforcement learning is very different from supervised machine learning. The latter uses a training data set which tells the machine what the output should be. This means that the machine is provided with the answer key to any problem. In reinforcement learning, there is no answer given to the machine. The machine must decide what it should do to achieve the result. Since there is no training data, the machine will learn from its experiences.

Let us look at the following example. There is an agent, and there is a reward. There are many hurdles between the agent or the machine and the reward. The machine or agent should identify the best path it should take to reach that reward. The following will explain this problem easily.

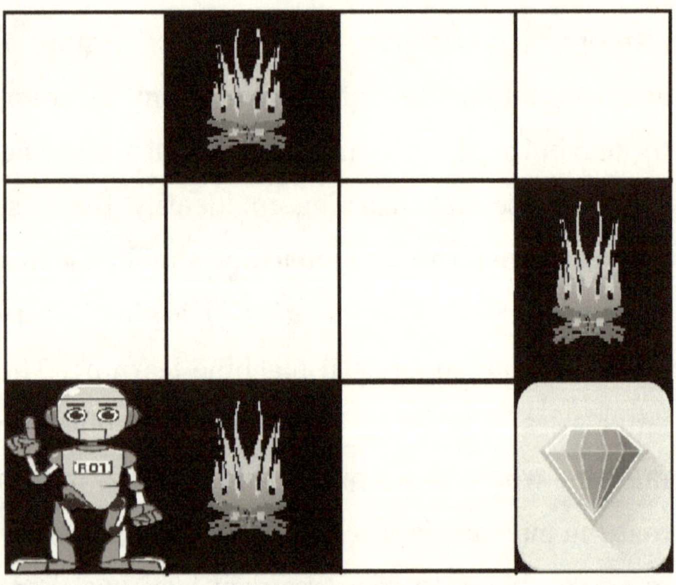

Reinforcement learning [ONLINE]. Available at:
https://www.geeksforgeeks.org/what-is-reinforcement-learning/
[Accessed 19 July 2019]

In the above image, there is a robot, fire and

diamond. The robot must find a way to get to the diamond by overcoming the hurdles. The robot will need to look at all the possible paths to reach the diamond, and choose the path that will let him reach the diamond with the least number of hurdles in his way. Every right step that the robot takes will reward him, and every incorrect step or move will deduct the reward. The full reward is calculated when the robot reaches the diamond.

Important Points of Reinforcement Learning

The following points will help you understand the process of reinforcement learning:

- **Input**: The input is the place or the state from which the model starts.

- **Output**: The model can take many outputs since there are many solutions to a specific problem.

- **Training**: The engineer can choose to

train the model on the basis of the input. The user can decide to reward or punish the model based on the state that the model returns to the user.

- **Learning**: The model will continue to learn.

- **Solution:** The model will identify the best solution based on the maximum reward that is calculated.

Types of Reinforcement

There are two types of reinforcement learning.

Positive

When an event occurs due to a specific behavior demonstrated by the machine, it will increase the frequency and strength of that behavior. In simple words, this type of reinforcement will have a positive effect on the model. The advantages of this type of reinforcement learning are:

- Sustains the changes made to the model for a long time Maximizes the performance of the model

The disadvantages of this type of learning are:

- Too many rewards can diminish the results since it will lead to an overload in the states.

Negative

Through negative reinforcement, the behavior is strengthened when a negative condition is avoided or stopped. The advantages of this type of learning are:

- Improves the performance of the model by allowing it to defy a method

- It will increase the frequency of the behavior

The disadvantage of this type of learning is:

- This will allow the model just to provide enough to meet the minimum behavior.

Chapter Four: Neural Networks

An artificial neural network is built to process information in the same way as the human brain. The key element of this network is how it is structured to process information. The network is composed of neurons, which are interconnected to process information. These neurons work together to solve problems. The neural network learns in the same way as the human brain—by example—and it is configured only for a specific application like data classification or pattern recognition through a process of learning. Learning in a biological system involves the adjustments that are made to the connections between the neurons. The same can be said for artificial neural networks.

Historical Background

The field of neural networks is not a new one, but the simulation of these networks has only gained popularity in recent years. Neural networks have survived at least one setback since their development.

Computer emulations have boosted some of the recent developments that have been made in the field of neural networks. When the concept of neural networks was introduced, many people threw themselves into research. However, they were unable to obtain enough information or data to help them use this concept to enhance the working of machines. This led to a dip in enthusiasm. Some researchers continued to study neural networks, and they developed technology that most people in the industry began to accept.

The artificial neural network was first produced in the year 1943 by Warren McCulloch and Walter Pitts. However, the technology that was available to them at that time did not allow them to work closely with a neural network.

Why Use Neural Networks?

You can use neural networks to detect trends and extract patterns from data that are often too complex for human beings to grasp and understand. Some computer programs and algorithms also find it difficult to understand or identify these trends. When a neural network is trained, it becomes an expert in that field. You can then use that network to predict the output for future input data and answer some important questions. Some of the other advantages include the following:

1. The networks use supervised machine learning and adapt to the tasks that are given to them.

2. A network can represent the information that it has been provided with during the learning stage.

3. The computations in a neural network run in parallel, and there are some devices that are being manufactured to use this attribute of neural networks.

4. When a neural network is damaged partially, it leads to a degradation in the performance of the network. That being said, there are some capabilities that the network will still retain even if it is damaged.

Neural Networks versus Conventional Computers

Neural networks and conventional computers do not use the same approach to solve a problem. Conventional computers often use algorithms to solve problems unless the system is aware of the steps it must follow to solve the problem. This restricts the computer's capabilities of solving problems that human beings understand and can solve. Computers are useful when they have been taught how to solve a problem that human beings cannot solve.

Neural networks function in the same way as the human brain. The network is made up of many neurons that are interconnected. These neurons work in parallel to solve specific problems. These networks learn by example, and they cannot be taught to perform specific tasks. The programmer must select the training data sets carefully. Otherwise, the network will never learn correctly how it must solve a problem since it will function incorrectly. The disadvantage of using a neural network is that the network often learns to solve problems that it has not been trained to solve, thereby making it unpredictable.

On the other hand, computers often use cognitive approaches to solve problems. The computer must know how it should solve the problem, and the user must state the problem without any ambiguous instructions. These instructions then get encrypted to a high-level programming language, which is then decoded into the machine's code. This process makes the machines predictable, and if there is an issue with the process, it is either a hardware or software issue.

Conventional computers and neural networks complement each other. Simple tasks like arithmetic calculations are suited to a conventional algorithmic computer while complex tasks are more suited to a neural network. Many tasks require a combination of both approaches to ensure that the machine performs at maximum efficiency.

The Architecture of Neural Networks

Feed-Forward Networks

In a feed-forward network, also known as a top-down or bottom-up network, the signals only travel in one direction—from the input layer to the output layer. There are no loops, so this means that the output values from one layer do not affect the output values in another layer. The network will always associate the input layer and the output layer. Pattern recognition uses this type of network.

Feedback Networks

A feedback network will allow a signal to travel in both directions, which introduces a feedback loop inside the network. These networks are complicated to build but are very powerful. The state of a feedback network will always change until it reaches an equilibrium point. The network will need to remain at this equilibrium until the data variables or points change. The network will then identify a new network. These networks are both recurrent and interactive, but only a single-layer network can be recurrent.

Network Layers

The most common type of neural network has three layers or groups of units. The first layer is an input layer that is connected to the hidden layer or unit. This hidden unit is connected to an output layer. The input layer represents the units of raw data or information that is provided to the neural network. It is the activity that takes place in the input layer that determines how the weights are placed on the neurons in the hidden layer. The weights and the values calculated by the neurons in the hidden layers define the behavior of the output layer. The weights that are placed on the nodes connecting the output layer to the hidden layer play a very important role.

The above-mentioned structure is a simple network, and the interesting thing about this network is that the hidden layer can choose to represent the output given by the input layer in any form. The weights that are placed on the nodes in the input layer will let the hidden layer know which nodes need to be active during the calculation. Therefore, any change made to the weights between the input and hidden nodes will allow the hidden layer to decide what data variables or points it should represent.

It is easy to distinguish between the architecture in a single-layer and multi-layer network. The former network is where every node is connected to another. This increases the computational power of the network. In the latter type of network, the layers are numbered instead of the nodes.

Perceptrons

It was in the 1960s that Frank Rosenblatt coined the term "perceptron." This was when some significant developments were being made in neural networks. This neural network follows the same structure as that of the MCP (McCulloch-Pitts) model. Every node in this network will be assigned a preprocessing, fixed, or additional weight. This network mimics the visual system in human beings, and it is for this reason that it is used to recognize patterns. They can, however, be used in many other applications.

Chapter Five: Deep Learning

From the first few chapters, we have gathered that the machine will use a training data set to understand different types of data and use that learning to predict the outcome for new data sets. Google and Facebook are, however, trying to identify words spoken and trying to categorize them. They are also trying to help different machines identify the relationship between different objects in the training data set, and assess that relationship between different variables or data points.

For example, if you want the computer to interpret "this is an elephant" exactly that way instead of "this is a collection of pixels," you must determine a way to map some features of the elephant to other complex features. For instance, you can convert a line, curve, pixels, sounds of alphabets and much more if you know how to transform the features of that entity into features that can be recognized by the machine. The machine can then use indexing or inference to predict the output. This type of learning is called deep learning.

Neural networks are used in deep learning models to identify the outputs. In this type of learning, different nodes are used as inputs in the different layers, and a signal from the input layer is sent to the hidden strata in the network. The hidden layers will use that input to calculate or derive the output. The work in deep learning is defined by how the human mind learns and how the mind learns. It also considers how calculations and computations take place in the cerebral cortex of the human brain.

Every node in the model is assigned a weight. For instance, if you are trying to use the model to identify or classify images, you can assign a weight to every pixel in the image that is used as the input. You should also include the output value that you want the machine to provide in the training data set. An error message is passed to the input layer or the source if the output image is not the same as the one in the training data set. This means that the weights assigned to the nodes will need to be updated.

The changes in these weights will help the user steer the network towards the right output. The signals sent from one side of the neural network to the other help the machine determine the right values that must be provided as the output. A system can use deep learning either in a supervised or unsupervised mode.

Supervised Modes

The neural network is taught with a training data set. In this type of learning, you will need to provide the output layer with the values that are associated with the input category. When a similar data set is used as the test data set, the network will look at the values present in the output layer, and use those values to provide the result to the user.

Unsupervised Modes

Both the input and the output layers in the network are provided with the examples that you are processing. Since the inner layers or hidden layers of the network are being compressed, most of the features in the data set are being overlooked. In this mode of learning, the network will use the values produced by the inner layer as the output.

Scientists and engineers are now spending the time to understand a deep learning system since it helps them identify the features that a network can support. This also helps the engineer or programmer understand how the different features in the data can be combined to derive the necessary output. One of the major disadvantages of using these methods is that they are hard to penetrate. It is hard for most systems to identify and report new features in the data set. This makes it extremely hard for the model to explain the method it used, which is an ability that a machine must possess. This means that the model can present you with some outputs or inferences that it may be unable to explain. You will need to dig deeper to understand the model and see how it derived a specific output.

Chapter Six: Algorithms

Linear Regression

Regression modeling is a powerful and elegant tool that is used by data scientists to estimate the value of the target variables if they are continuous. Different models are used of which the linear regression model is the simplest of all. This model uses a straight line to identify and quantify a relationship between a single continuous predictor variable and response variable. There are also multiple regression models where numerous predictor variables can be used to estimate one response.

Apart from linear and multiple regression models, there is a least squared regression model that is being used now since it is a powerful tool. There is a level of disparity that lies between the assumptions of each of these models and it is important that the assumptions are always validated before a model is built. If the data scientist were to build a model that was based on assumptions that were not verified, this could lead to failures that would cause damage to the scientist and the machine being used.

When the user has obtained the desired results from the model, he or she will need to ensure that no linear relationship exists between the different variables in the model. There could be a relationship that exists that is granular and difficult to identify. There is, however, a systematic approach to determining whether there is any linear relationship between the variables, and that is using inference. Four inferential methods could be used to determine the relationship:

- The confidence interval for the slope, β_1

- The prediction interval for a random value of the response variable given a value of the predictor

- The confidence interval for the mean of the response variable given a value of the predictor

- The t-test to assess the relationship that exists between the predictor and response variable

The methods described above depend on how well the data adheres to the assumptions made before beginning the process of modeling. There are two graphical methods used to understand how well the data adheres to the assumptions or the bases – a normal plot based on probabilities or a plot that is based on residuals against predicted or fitted values. A quantile-quantile plot that plots the quantiles derived from a given distribution against the quantiles from a normal distribution is called a normal probability plot. This plot will determine if the specified or selected distribution deviates from the normal distribution. In this plot, the values from the chosen distribution are plotted and compared against the values of the normal distribution. The points in a normal distribution will always be present on the vertical line. Any variations in the linearity of the points from the chosen distribution will lead to non-normality. We will need to evaluate if the regression assumptions hold true by verifying if there are any patterns that exist in the residual versus the fit plot. If there is a variation, we can say that the assumptions have been violated. If there is no obvious variation, the assumptions are still intact.

If the plots that you have obtained do violate the assumptions, you can apply a transformation function to the variables in the data set. You can also use these functions if the points in the data set do not have a linear relationship.

Multiple Regression

Regression modeling can use both single variables and multiple variables. In the previous section, we looked at simple linear regression where a single predictor and response variable are selected. Data scientists are only interested in the relationship that exists between predictor variables and target variables. Applications built for data scientists include large data sets that include hundreds, maybe thousands, of variables that have a relationship with the response or the target variable. This is where the data scientist would prefer to use multiple regression models that would provide improved accuracy and increase the precision of prediction and estimation. This is like the improved accuracy of regression estimates over bivariate or univariate estimates.

Multiple linear regression models use linear surfaces like hyperplanes or planes to determine the relationship between a set of predictor variables and one continuous target or response variable. Predictor variables are often continuous, but there could be categorical predictor variables included in the model using dummy or indicator variables. In a simple linear regression model, a straight line of dimension one is used to estimate the relationship between one predictor and the response variable. If we were to evaluate the relationship between two predictor variables and one response variable, we must use a plane to estimate it because a plane is a linear surface in two dimensions.

Data scientists must identify ways to understand multicollinearity, which is a condition where some predictor variables are correlated. This will lead to an instability in the solution set that is extracted leading to some incoherent results. For example, if there is severe multicollinearity in a data set, the F-test can be used to obtain the required result. But, the t-test which is the test that is often used cannot be used since the predictors are irrelevant.

The estimates that are produced for different regression coefficients that represent different samples of the data have a high variability. There could be situations where different samples could produce some estimates that are widely different. For instance, a given sample can provide a positive estimate for the variable x1, but another sample can provide a negative sample for that same variable. This is a situation that you must avoid since it is important to identify the relationship between the predictor and response variables. The analyst should investigate and analyze the data to understand the correlation structure that exists between the different predictor variables. You should ignore the target variables.

Let us make an assumption that we do not want to identify the correlation that exists between the predictor variables, but still went ahead with the regression algorithm. Would there be a way to identify whether there is multicollinearity in the data? Yes. We will need to look at the variance inflation factors that will show which variable is multicollinear. You must remember that you need to standardize or normalize the variables that are involved to remove or reduce the probability that the variability in one variable will affect the value of other variables.

Logistic Regression

Logistic regression is used to identify the relationship that exists between a set of predictor variables and a continuous or categorical response variable. This response variable is often categorical. For such cases, linear regression is not appropriate, but the analyst can turn to an analogous method, logistic regression, which is like the linear regression model in many ways. In this type of regression, the relationship between the variables is described.

One of the most attractive properties of linear regression is that closed-form solutions for the optimal values of the regression coefficients can be obtained by the least-squares method. Unfortunately, no such closed-form solution can be found to estimate the coefficients in logistic regression. Therefore, we will need to use the maximum likelihood estimation method to estimate the values of the parameters. These values should maximize the equation.

The maximum likelihood estimators can be found by differentiating the likelihood function, L (β|x), with respect to each parameter and then setting the resulting forms to be equal to zero. Unfortunately, unlike linear regression, closed-form solutions for these differentiations are not available. Therefore, other methods, such as iterative weighted least squares, must be applied.

The linear regression method is used to identify and establish a relationship between a set of predictor variables and a discrete or continuous response variable. Logistic regression provides the machine with some methods that it can use to describe the relationship that exists between a set of predictor variables and a categorical response variable. In this type of regression, it is assumed that there is a nonlinear relationship between the predictor and response variable. The response variable used in linear regression is a random variable that has a conditional mean. In logistic regression, the conditional mean takes on a different form.

Bayesian Networks and Naïve Bayes Estimation

In the field of statistics, the probability is approached in two ways – the classical approach or the Bayesian approach. Probability is often taught using the classical approach or the frequentist approach. This is a method that is followed in all beginner's classes in statistics. In this approach, every parameter is assigned a fixed value which is unknown. These prospective values are termed as the relative frequencies for various categories. The experiment is repeated for each of these categories an indefinite number of times. For example, if you toss a coin twenty times, you can expect to observe heads 80% of the time. You can, however, be certain that you will obtain heads at least 50% of the time. This is the behavior that defines the prospect of this approach.

There are some situations, however, where is makes it hard for anyone to understand this situation because of how probability is defined. For instance, can you calculate the probability that a terrorist will attack New York city using a bomb? Since such an instance has already occurred, it will be easy to calculate the long-term behavior of this situation. Alternatively, you can use the frequentist approach where you have a list of fixed parameters, and you can use those parameters to assess the randomness in the data set. This randomness is considered the random sample in the distribution.

These assumptions are changed in the Bayesian approach. In the Bayesian approach, every parameter present in the data set is a random variable. These parameters are assumed to have come from a specific distribution that has some values. Through this approach, the machine can identify the values of the parameters by calculating the mean and variances of the distribution.

Most experts are skeptical when it comes to using the Bayesian approach for the following reasons:

1. A prior distribution may or may not have been specified. Even if a distribution has been provided, two experts can suggest different distributions. This will lead to the generation of two posterior distributions. The solution to this issue is to always use a large volume of data to choose the non-informative prior. If this cannot be done, the posterior distribution can be calculated using two different prior distributions. The machine can then test the goodness of fit of the data and choose the better model.

2. You cannot use the Bayesian approach in a data mining problem when there are issues with scalability. This is because the Bayesian approach cannot be used on a data set that has too many dimensions. If you want to normalize the parameters, you will need to integrate over every possible value of the parameter. This is hard to do, but the introduction of the Markov chain Monte Carlo method has helped to cope with this issue.

Clustering

This section provides information on clustering which is an unsupervised machine learning algorithm. In the third chapter, we learned that an unsupervised algorithm would learn to make some inferences about and from an unlabeled data set. The objective of an unsupervised algorithm is to understand every variable and data point in the data set with the help of the training data set. In a supervised machine learning algorithm, we are always looking for an answer based on what the input data set is. In unsupervised machine learning, we provide the model with the input data set and look at how the model interprets the information.

In the data science domain, you always look at how the available data can be used to predict the output of some similar data sets. There will be times when you want to divide the data points into distinct categories and use those categories to make the predictions. The former is an example of supervised machine learning while the latter is an example of unsupervised machine learning.

Consider the following example – you are now working at a pizza outlet, and you are asked by your manager to create a feature that will help you manage the orders. This feature should allow you to predict the time you will take to deliver the order to the customer. There is some historical information that you have been provided with to help you calculate this time. You will be given the distance that the delivery executive travels and some other necessary parameters. You can use this information to help you predict the delivery time for future orders. This is a classic example of supervised machine learning.

Now, let us look at a different requirement. You are still working at the pizza joint, but you now need to identify the group of customers you should target to run the coupon campaign. There is some historical data that is available which provides information about the customers, their address, age and other information. You can use that information to classify the customers into various categories based on some factors. You can then make the necessary predictions using those categories. This is an example of an unsupervised machine learning algorithm since you are not making predictions based on some customer clusters.

Let us now look at a requirement. You are employed at the same pizza joint, but you are tasked with identifying the segment of your customers to run a coupon campaign. You have access to some historical data such as the name of your customers, their age, area and other information. You can now classify these customers into different clusters based on numerous factors. This is an example of unsupervised machine learning why you are not predicting by nearly categorizing your customers into numerous groups.

Real Life Applications of Clustering

The clustering algorithm is used in many domains including those domains with some complex and large data sets like genomics. In genomics, the model will create a cluster of the genes if they have similar properties. This algorithm is also used in astronomy to classify different celestial objects and stars using factors like color, distance, size, material, etc. You can also use clustering to predict earthquakes using the epicenters of the areas or zones. Businesses also use this algorithm for the following reasons:

- In driving targeted advertisements

- Medical image detection

- Market segmentation

- Image segmentation

- In Netflix recommendations

- Anomaly detection

- Social media analysis

- Recommendation engines

- Search result grouping etc.

Decision Trees

A decision tree is one of the most powerful classification algorithms that was developed. This is a supervised machine learning algorithm and will work on both categorical and continuous data. You can use this algorithm to predict the category or the class of any input data. Another popular classification algorithm is the k-nearest algorithm. The objective of this algorithm is to develop a model that can predict the target variable for any input data set using a decision rule. These rules can be mentioned to the model during the training phase or can be inferred by the model.

In simple words, this algorithm is similar to the conditional statements which are used in most programming languages. The decision tree has a different syntax or format when compared to a conditional statement. This is a branch based or flow chart type of system and is an algorithm that any person can understand or follow. Consider the following example – you receive an email and based on some conditions or the subject you classify that email as spam or important. You can develop an application that can perform the same function. If you want to use a machine, you can give the model some predefined rules that it must follow.

The decision tree is a tree, and you can use any branch to obtain the output or answer to any given question. You can answer these questions using all the information that is present at the nodes. The branches will represent the course of action or the path that the machine can take. The image below will show you how you can use a tree to answer a real question.

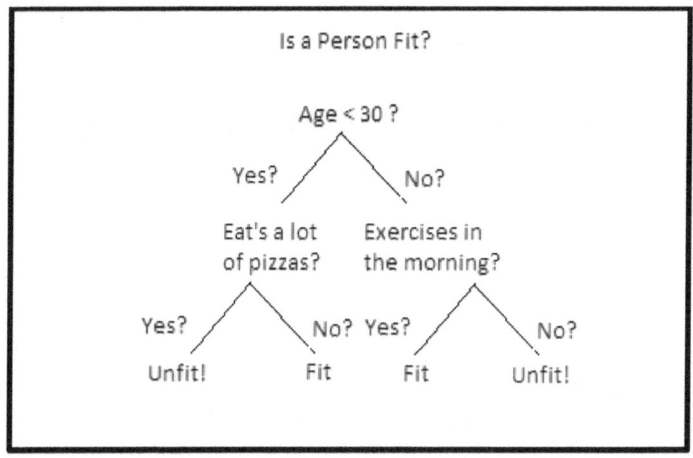

Reinforcement learning [ONLINE]. Available at: https://www.xoriant.com/blog/product-engineering/decision-trees-machine-learning-algorithm.html [Accessed 22July 2019]

Chapter Seven: Basics of Python Programming

Running Python

Python is a tool or software that can be installed and run on multiple operating systems including Mac OS X, or OS/2, Linux, Unix and Windows. Python is already installed in your system if you use the GNU/Linux or Mac OS X operating systems. Experts suggest that you use this type of a system since Python is already set up. The programs in this book work on any operating system.

Installing on Windows

If you use Windows, you will first need to install Python, after which you will need to configure some settings. Ensure that you do this before you begin to use the codes in this book. To make the necessary changes, you will need to check the instructions provided for your operating system, and follow them word for word. You can use the following pages for the same:

https://wiki.python.org/moin/BeginnersGuide/Download

https://docs.python.org/3/faq/windows.html

If you're using OS X, your instructions are here:

https://www.python.org/downloads/mac-osx/

You will first need to download the official installer. Alternative versions for AMD and Itanium machines are available at https://www.python.org/downloads/. This file, which has a .msi extension, must be saved at a location which you can find easily. You should then click on the Python installation wizard. This will take over the installation process. It is recommended that you use the default settings if you do not know what the answers may be.

Choosing the Right Version

Different installers include different numbers after the word Python which refers to the version number. If you look at the archives on multiple websites, the version numbers will range from 2.5.2 to 3.0 where the former is an old but usable version of Python while the latter is the latest version. The Python team released the version 2.6 at the same time that it released the version 3.0. This is because there are some people who may still want to stick to version 2 of Python since they want to continue to write code the old way but still want to benefit from general fixes and some of the new features introduced in version 3.0.

Python is continuously evolving, and the latest version of this software is the version 3.1.1. You must keep in mind that these new versions are the same as version 3.0 with some refinements. Therefore, the newer versions will continue to be referred to as 3.0 in this book. Version 3.0

includes several changes to the programming language that is incompatible with version 2.0. You do not have to worry about programming using different versions of Python since there is only a subtle difference in the language or syntax.

Python may run differently on different operating systems, but we will not be covering that aspect since that is outside the scope of this book. The codes in the book will work in the same way across different operating systems. This is one of the many good points of Python. If you wish to learn more about Python, you should read the documentation prepared by the developers which are free and well-written. It is available on at http://www.Python.org/doc/.

Getting Started

When you sit down to write a new program, you must remember that it starts with a problem.

Before you write code for anything, you have to develop an idea of what it is that you would like to create and the problem that you are looking to solve. This will help you develop a fair idea of how you would like to solve the problem.

Over the course of the next chapter, we will look at the software development cycle which will help you through the process of designing the software. This is a step that most people will need to learn separately since most programming guides usually switch to the intricacies of the language and focus on how to develop code which can make it difficult for a beginner to understand how to understand the code and what needs to be done to fix that code.

Understanding the principles of software design can dramatically speed up the process of creating new software and help ensure that important details are not missed out.

In the subsequent chapters, you will learn to build the designs and ideas in Python and learn to construct the basic units of the codes using words, data and numbers. You will also learn how to manipulate these inputs to refine the code. It is important to learn how to compare different sets of data to make informed decisions. Over the course of the book, you will learn to refine the designs you have created and break them down into portions that can be coded easily. These steps will help to expand your understanding of the language and help you turn your ideas into complete computer programs.

Creating your Own Files

Python is described as a self-documenting language which does not mean that the user manual is written for you by Python. However, you can add documentation strings, which are defined as blocks of text, to your script or code. These documentation strings will show up when you open your code which can then be turned into web pages that provide useful references to those looking for similar code. An example of documentation strings has been provided in the subsequent chapters and it is important to learn to include documentation strings in your code at an early stage.

In the last chapter, we learned that an identifier is a part of a variable, which is a unit of data. These variables and identifiers are held in the computer's memory and its value can be changed by making a modification to a value that is already present in the variable. This chapter will introduce you to the different types of variables that you can use when writing a program in Python. You will also learn how these variables can be used to convert your designs into working codes using Python. This is when you begin real programming. Over the course of this chapter, we will work on two programs – one where we will learn to format and manipulate text strings and another to perform a simple mathematical calculation.

The programs mentioned above can be written easily using different variables. When you use variables, you can specify a function, method of calculation that must be used to obtain a solution without the knowledge of the type of value that the variable must refer to in advance. Every piece of information that must be put into a system needs to be converted into a variable, before the interpreter uses it in the function. The output of the program is obtained once the interpreter runs the contents or the values of the variables through the functions in the program.

Choosing the Right Identifier

Every section of your code is identified using an identifier. The compiler or editor in Python will consider any word that is delimited by quotation marks, has not been commented out, or has escaped in a way by which it cannot be considered or marked as an identifier. Since an identifier is only a name label, it could refer to just about anything; therefore, it makes sense to have names that can be understood by the language. You have to ensure that you do not choose a name that has already been used in the current code to identify any new variable.

If you choose a name that is the same as the older name, the original variable becomes inaccessible. This can be a bad idea if the name chosen is an essential part of your program. Luckily, when you write a code in Python, it does not let you name a variable with a name used already. The next section of this chapter lists out the important words, also called keywords, in Python which will help you avoid the problem.

Python Keywords

The following words, also called keywords, are the base of the Python language. You cannot use these words to name an identifier or a variable in your program since these words are considered the core words of the language. These words cannot be misspelled and must be written in the same way for the interpreter to understand what you want the system to do. Some of the words listed below have a different meaning which will be covered in later chapters.

- False
- None
- assert
- True
- as
- break
- continue
- def
- import
- in
- is
- and
- class
- del
- or
- from
- global
- raise
- return

- else

- elif

- not

- or

- pass

- except

- try

- while

- with

- finally

- if

- lambda

- nonlocal

- yield

Understanding the Naming Convention

Let us talk about the words that you can use and those you cannot use. Every variable name must always begin with an underscore or a letter. Some variable names can have numbers in them, but no variable name can begin with a number. If the interpreter comes across a set of variables that begin with a number instead of quotation marks or a letter, it will only consider that variable as a number. You should never use anything other than an underscore, number or letter to identify a variable in your code. You must also remember that Python is a case-sensitive language; therefore false and False are two different entities. The same can be said for vvariable, Vvariable and VVariable. As a beginner, you must make a note of all the variables you use in your code. This will also help you find something easier in your code.

Creating and Assigning Values to Variables

Every variable is created in two stages – the first is to initialize the variable and the second is to assign a value to that variable. In the first step, you must create a variable and name it appropriately to stick a label on it and in the second step; you must put a value in the variable. These steps are performed using a single command in Python using the equal to sign. When you must assign a value, you should write the following code:

Variable = value

Every section of the code that performs some function, like an assignment, is called a statement. The section of the code that is used to obtain the value of the variable is called an expression. Let us take a look at the following example:

Length = 14

Breadth = 10

Height = 10

Area_Triangle = Length * Breadth * Height

Any variable can be assigned a value or an expression, like the assignment made to

Area_Triangle in the example above.

Every statement must be written in a separate line. If you write the statements down the way you would write down a shopping list, you are going the right way. Every recipe begins in the same way with a list of ingredients and the proportions along with the equipment that you would need to use to complete your dish. The same happens when you write a Python code – you first define the variables you want to use and then create functions and methods to use on those variables.

Recognizing Different Types of Variables

The interpreter in Python recognizes different types of variables – sequences or lists, numbers, words or string literals, Booleans and mappings. These variables are often used in Python programs. A variable None has a type of its own called NoneType. Before we look at how words and numbers can be used in Python, we must first look at the dynamic typing features in Python.

Working with Dynamic Typing

When you assign a value to a variable, the interpreter will choose to decide the type of value the variable is which is called dynamic typing. This type of typing does not have anything to do with how fast you can type on the keyboard. Unlike the other languages, Python does not require that the user declare the types of the variables being used in the program. This can be considered both a blessing and a curse. The advantage is that you do not have to worry about the variable type when you write the code, and you only need to worry about the way the variable behaves.

Dynamic Typing in Python makes it easier for the interpreter to handle user input that is unpredictable. The interpreter for Python accepts different forms of user input to which it assigns a dynamic type which means that a single statement which you can use to deal with words, numbers or data types. You as a user do not have to know what the data type the variable must be. Not needing to declare any variable when you use it will make you want to introduce variables at random places in your scripts. You must remember that Python won't complain unless you try to use a variable before you have actually assigned it a value, but it's really easy to lose track of what variables you are using and where you set up their values in the script.

There are two really sensible practices that will help keep you sane when you start to create large numbers of different variables. One is to set up a bunch of default values at the start of each section if you are sure of where you will need to use them. It is always a good idea to group all the variables together. The other is to keep track of the expected types and values of your variables, keeping a data table in your design document for each program that you are writing.

The API in Python will need to keep track of the variable type for the following reasons. The machine will need to set some memory aside to store this information. The different data types in Python take up different volumes of space. The second reason is that keeping track of types helps to avoid and troubleshoot errors. Once Python has decided what type a variable is, it will flag up a TypeError if you try to perform an inappropriate operation on that data. Although this might at first seem to be an unnecessary irritation, you will discover that this can be an incredibly useful feature of Python. Let us look at the command-line example below:

b = 3

c = 'word'

trace = False

b + c

Traceback (most recent call last): File "", line 1, in

<module>

TypeError: unsupported operand type(s) for +: 'int' and 'str'

c - trace

Traceback (most recent call last):

File "", line 1, in <module>

TypeError: unsupported operand type(s) for -: 'str' and 'bool'

The program written above will perform the operation on those data types which are not compatible with each other. You're not allowed to include a word or number, or take a yes/no answer away from it. It is necessary to convert the data to a compatible type before trying to process it. You can add words together or take numbers away from each other, just like you can in real life, but you can't do arithmetic on a line of text. Python will alert you if there is some error in your logic using tracebacks. In this case, it gives you the TypeError. This error will let you know that you must rewrite the code to ensure that you let the compiler know what type of information you should put in. This information is dependent on the output that you want to obtain.

The purpose of data types is to allow us to represent information that exists in the real world, that is, the world that exists outside your computer, as opposed to the virtual world inside. We can have the existential conversation about what is real and what is not some other time. The previous example uses variables of type int (whole numbers) and type str (text). It will quickly become apparent that these basic data types can only represent the simplest units of information; you may need to use quite a complicated set of words, numbers, and relationships to describe even the simplest real-world entity in virtual-world terms.

Python provides many ways of combining these simple data types to create more complex data types, which I'll come to later in this book. First, you must learn more about the fundamental building blocks that are used to define your data and the basic set of actions you can use to manipulate the different types of values.

The None Variable

A predefined variable called None is a special value in Python. This variable has a type of its own and is useful when you need to create a variable but not define or specify a value to that variable. When you assign values such as "" and 0, the interpreter will define the variable as the str or int variable.

Information = None

A variable can be assigned the value None using the statement above. The next few examples will use real-world information that will be modeled into a virtual form using some fantasy characters. This example uses some statistics to represent some attributes of the characters to provide data for the combat system. You can use this example to automate your database and your accounts. So, let us take a look at some of the characters in the example.

In the program, hello_world.py, you saw how you can get a basic output using the print () function. You can use this function to print out the value of the variable and a literal string of characters. Often, each print statement must start off on a new line, but several values can be printed on a single line by using a comma to separate them; print () can then be used to concatenate all the variables into a single line only separated by spaces.

Race = "Goblin"

Gender = "Female"

print (Gender, Race) Female Goblin

Different segments of information can be combined into a single line using multiple methods. Some of these methods are more efficient when compared to others. Adjacent strings that are not separated will be concatenated automatically, but this is not a function that works for most variables.

>>> print ("Male" "Elf")

The expression above will give you the following output – "MaleElf" However, when you enter the following code, >>> print ("Male" Race)

You will receive the following error:

File "<stdin>", line 1

print ("Male" Race)

^

SyntaxError: invalid syntax

This approach cannot be used since you cannot write a string function as a variable and a string together since this is just a way of writing a single line string.

Working with Numbers

You can always assign a number to a variable.

Muscle = 8

Brains = 13

If any variable begins with a number, the interpreter will view that variable as a number, even if there are some other characters used in that variable. It is for this reason that you should never name a variable starting with a number. There are a few points that you will need to keep in mind before you work with numbers.

Computers Only Take Zeros and Ones

The information on any computer is stored only as a binary value - zero or one. A machine will always store and process any volume of data using switches that are labeled as zero or one.

Using Boolean

As mentioned earlier, a computer can only register two values – True (value = 1) and False (value = 0). These values are known as Boolean operators and can be manipulated using operators like OR, NOT and AND. These operators are explained in further detail in the following chapter. Boolean values can be assigned as follows:

Mirage = False

Intelligence = True

Using Whole Numbers

Whole numbers, also called integers, do not have decimal points and can be zero, positive and negative.

These numbers are used to refer to different things like the recipe example mentioned above.

Performing Basic Mathematical Operations

Now that you know how to store data in a variable let us take a look at how to manipulate that data. Basic mathematical operations can be performed using operators like +, - and *. These operators create an expression that must be evaluated before you can obtain a value. The following statements can be used to perform these operations

>>>muscle = 2 + 3

>>>brains = 7+4

speed = 5 * 6

weirdness = muscle * brains + speed

weirdness

All these operations work using the BODMAS mathematical algorithm.

Working with Floats and Fractions

Python allows you to express a fraction using the float data type since you can use decimal points. These numbers can be positive or negative. You do not have to specify if a variable is float when you declare it, because Python will convert any number with a decimal in it to the float data type.

Muscle = 2.8

Brains = 4.6

Speed = 6.8

Even if there is a zero before and after the decimal point in the number, it is considered a fraction. You can manipulate this data type by using a mathematical operation that is given above.

Converting Data Types

There are many functions that you can use to convert the data type from one to another in Python. The data types that users often use are:

- int (x) – used to convert any number into an integer float (x) – used to convert a number to a float data type

- str (object) – convert any type into a string

that can be used to print

float (23)

23.0

int (23.5)

23

float (int (23.5))

23 Loops

While Statement result = 1

while result < 1000: result *= 2

print result

To control the number of times the loop is processed, it is necessary specify or include the conditional expression. The loop will continue to run as long as the expression holds true at the start of the iteration. In the preceding example, our conditional expression is result < 1000. So, as long as the value of result is less than 1,000, the loop will continue processing. Once result reaches 1,024 (210), the code in the body of the loop will not be processed by the interpreter.

The variables used in the conditional expression are often expendable entities, which are only required for as long as the loop is active. Rather than keep thinking up different names, this kind of integer counter is usually named i or j by convention.

Two things are important to remember in this sort of construction: Any variable used in the conditional expression must be initialized before the execution of the loop. Also, there must be some way of updating this variable within the loop; otherwise, the loop will just go around and around forever, which is called an infinite loop.

It is possible to use different sorts of variables in the conditional expression. Let's consider the problem of calculating the average of several numbers input by the user. The main problem here is that I don't know how many numbers will be input. The solution is to use what is called a sentinel value to control the loop. Rather than using the counter in this instance, the script checks the value of the user input number. While it is positive (i.e., >= 0) the loop processes as normal, but as soon as a negative number is entered, the loop is broken, and the script goes on to calculate the average. Let us take a look at the following example:

```
counter = 0

total = 0

number = 0

while number >= 0:

number = int (input ("Enter a positive number\nor a negative to exit: "))

total += number

counter += 1

average = total / counter

print(average)
```

There are several methods of getting out of loops cleanly, the chief ones being the use of the break and continue keywords: If you want to get out of a loop without executing any more statements in the loop body, use a break. If you just want to get out of the iteration, and move onto the next iteration of the loop.

At times, you will want the interpreter to recognize a condition but do nothing. In this case, the pass keyword can be useful; it creates a null statement, which simply tells the interpreter to go to the next instruction.

Nesting Loops

Python allows you to nest conditional statements and loops. You can always build an infinite loop, but it is always a good idea to restrict the number of iterations. This is because it is easy to forget the option that the program is looking at during an iteration. If you have too many blocks within a main block of code, it will be hard for others to understand the code, even if you do include comments. This is also considered a bad writing style. If you have come up with a design that involves two or three layers of looping, you should probably start thinking about redesigning it to avoid the excessive depth of nesting.

For

Another control statement that you should learn more about is the 'for' statement. This statement is constructed similarly to the if and while statements. Its construction is for an element in sequence: followed by an indented suite of instructions. During the loop's first iteration, the variable element contains the first element in the sequence and is available to the indented suite. During the second iteration, it contains the second element in the sequence, and so on.

To learn more about how the statement works, you must understand sequences. A sequence is a series of individual objects or values. One of the simplest sequences in Python is a string. A string is a series of individual characters including punctuation and spaces. The other types of sequences are lists and tuples. A tuple and a list are sequences of variables or data items, and the difference between the two is that you can edit a list, but you cannot edit a tuple. You can use both in the 'for' statement.

```
# tuple

sequence1 = (1, 2, 3)

# list

sequence2 = [1, 2, 3]
```

Items in Sequences

Indices can be used to fetch individual or single items in a sequence. The index will define the position of a specific item or element in a given sequence. This index is a whole number and is specified in square brackets following the name of the variable. So, s[i] will retrieve the item at position i of sequence s. This allows you to access a single character in a string:

vegetable = 'pumpkin'

vegetable [0]

'p'

Or an item in a list:

>>>vegetable = ['pumpkins', 'potatoes', 'onions', 'eggplant']

>>>vegetable [1]

'pumpkins'

You will notice that indexing always begins at zero. This means that an index of [3] will retrieve the fourth item in the list, since the first item is always referenced with the index [0]. You can, therefore, use integers zero through to one less the number of the variables in the sequence. The negative index will look at the variables from the end of the list.

>>>vegetable [-1]

'eggplant'

Slices can be used to grab the different sections in any sequence. You can use this method to fetch many items in a sequence. A slice is written using the same notation as an index. The only difference is that the integers are separated by a colon. The first value is the starting point, and this value is included. The second number in the notation is the end point of the slice, and it is exclusive. If you look at s[0:2], the compiler will slice the list from the variable with the index zero and stop exactly before the variable with the index two.

You do not necessarily have to use the third value, and this is an additional step. This can be negative; therefore you can retrieve all the other items instead of picking this item from the sequential list. Alternatively, you can retrieve items backward as well. So, s [i: j: step] will give you the slice that begins from the variable i, but will not include the variable j. Here, s is the sequence.

If you ignore the initial point, the slice will always start at the beginning of the sequence. If you forget the end, the slice will continue to the last variable in the original or main sequence.

Slicing and indexing do not change the original sequence. They will develop a new sequence. The actual data items in the sequence will be the same. So, if you want to modify an individual item in the sequence, you will see that the item has changed in the slice as well.

Tuples

Tuples are a group of items or elements that are ordered and immutable. You should think of a tuple as a sealed packet of information.

A tuple is specified as a comma-separated list of values. These values can be enclosed within parentheses if necessary. In some cases, these parentheses are required, so always use them regardless of whether or not you think they are necessary. The values in the tuple do not necessarily have to be of the same data type. Some values can also be other tuples.

Creating a Tuple

Tuples can be created with no items in it using the round brackets ().

>>>empty_tuple= ()

If you want only one item in the tuple, you should enter the first item followed by a comma.

>>>one_item = ('blue',)

Changing Values in a Tuple

The values in a tuple cannot be changed by any user. These tuples are sealed packets of information that are often used in situations where a set of values need to be passed on from one location to another. If you wish to change the sequence of the data, you should use a list.

List

A list is an ordered, comma-separated list of items enclosed in square brackets. Items in the list do not have to be of the same data type. An item can also be another list.

You can slice, concatenate and index lists just like you would with any other sequence. You can always change the individual items in a list when compared to a string or a tuple. Lists are more flexible when compared to tuples. You can always assign data to the slices, thereby changing the size of the list or clearing it fully.

Creating a List

It is easy to create a list.

shopping_list = ['detergent', 'deodorant', 'shampoo', 'body wash'] Modifying a List

A new value can be added to a list using the assignment operator.

shopping_list [1] = 'candles'

shopping_list

['detergent', 'candles', 'deodorant', 'shampoo', 'body wash'] Stacks and Queues

Lists contain the ordered data points, and it is easy to use them to store any ordered information. You can do this by using either stacks or queues. A stack follows the last in first out structure (LIFO) and is analogous to the discarded pile of cards in a card game. You can add items into the stack using the list.append() function, and remove them using the pop() function. You should note that there are no index arguments, so the item that is at the bottom of the list will be removed or popped.

shopping_list.append ('brush')

shopping_list.pop()

'candles'

>>> shopping_list

['detergent', 'deodorant', 'shampoo', 'body wash']

In the other approach, you will create a structure that follows the first in, first out (FIFO) structure like a queue. This process works like a pipe, where you will need to push the items from one end of the pipe, and the item that was first sent into the pipe comes out of the pipe. You can always push items into the pipe using the append() function and retrieve or remove them using the pop() function. This time, you will need to include the index to ensure that you remove the correct item from the queue.

shopping_list.append ('brush')

shopping_list.pop(0) 'detergent'

shopping_list

['deodorant', 'shampoo', 'body wash', 'brush]'

Dictionaries

A dictionary is like an address book. For instance, if you know the name of a person, you can use the address book to obtain the details about that person. The name is the key, and the information about the key is the value. The name or the key should always be of an immutable type, like a tuple, string or number, and the value can be whatever you want it to be. Since dictionaries are a mutable data type, you can always modify, remove or add the pairs. The keys are always mapped to some specific objects, and it is for this reason that we often use a dictionary to map information in Python.

The dictionary can be used to store those attributes and values that define or describe a concept or entity. For instance, you can use the dictionary to count the instances of a specific object or state. This is because every key in the dictionary will have a unique identifier, and this key can be used to store the input data points, and the value can be used to store the outputs or results.

Install Packages Required for Machine Learning Applications

There are some packages that you will need to install before you begin working on building the machine learning model mentioned in the next few chapters. These packages contain numerous features and functions that you can use at different times when building the machine learning model.

Open a terminal and Run the following commands

pip install numpy

pip install SciPy

pip install SciKit-learn

pip install matplotlib

```
pip install pandas
```

You should open a Python script and write the code given below. Alternatively, you can open the terminal and then type Python in the command prompt. Once the interpreter opens, you should type the following code and test if the packages that you need are installed accurately.

Sample Code

Check the versions of libraries

Python version

```
import sys
print('Python: {}'.format(sys.version))
scipy import scipy
print('scipy: {}'.format(scipy.__version__))
numpy
import numpy
print('numpy: {}'.format(numpy.__version__))
matplotlib import matplotlib
print('matplotlib:
```

```
{}'.format(matplotlib.__version__))
```

pandas

```
import pandas
```

```
print('pandas: {}'.format(pandas.__version__))
```

SciKit-learn import sklearn

```
print('sklearn: {}'.format(sklearn.__version__))
```

The output for the above script must look something like this on the terminal: Output

Python: 2.7.11 (default, Mar 1 2016, 18:40:10)

[GCC 4.2.1 Compatible Apple LLVM 7.0.2 (clang-700.1.81)] SciPy: 0.17.0

numpy: 1.10.4

matplotlib: 1.5.1

pandas: 0.17.1

sklearn: 0.18.1

Once these packages are installed, you should open the terminal, create the script, import the packages, read the documentation and then play around with a few basic functions to understand these packages better.

Libraries in Python

In this section, you will learn about the different libraries in Python that you can use when you build a deep neural network. The list of libraries in this chapter is not exhaustive.

Keras

Keras is a modular and minimalist neural network library that uses either TensorFlowor Theano as its backend. Keras allows you to experiment quickly, which means that you can obtain results for many problems fast. It is easy to build a neural network in Keras since it includes the best optimizers, normalizers and activation functions. Keras focuses more on Convolutional Neural Networks.

In Keras, you can construct graph-based and sequence-based networks, which makes it easier to implement architectures like SqueezeNet and GoogleNet easier. The only problem with Keras is that it does not allow the engineer to train multiple networks or layers in parallel since it does not support a multi-GPU environment. The examples in later chapters use the Keras libraries to build a neural network in Python.

Theano

If Theano was not developed, it would have been difficult for engineers to experiment with higher-level abstraction problems. At its very core, Theano is a library that an engineer can use to define, optimize and evaluate some complex mathematical expressions that include multi-dimensional arrays. Theano can achieve this since it supports the use of GPUs. Experts believe that Theano is the building block for neural networks in Python. Therefore, it can be integrated with different libraries to build better and complex models.

TensorFlow

TensorFlow is a library that is similar to Theano. It is an open source library which is used for numerical computation. This library was developed by a research team in Google's Machine Intelligence organization. Through TensorFlow, an engineer can distribute the computing function of the network between multiple GPUs. You can use TensorFlow as a backend for Keras when you build deep neural networks in Python.

SciKit-Learn

Scikit-learn is a Python library that is open source. You can use this library to implement different machine learning, visualization, cross-validation and pre-processing algorithms. You can do this through a unified interface. Let us look at some features of SciKit-learn:

- The efficient and simple tools for data analysis and data mining. These tools include clustering algorithm, support vector machines, gradient boosting, random forests, k-means, classification and regression algorithms. The tools can be used by anybody and in any context.

- This is built using the matplotlib, SciPy and NumPy libraries.

Chapter Eight: How to Clean Data Using Python

Most engineers and data scientists spend too much of their time in cleaning a dataset, and manipulating that data into a format that they can use to train the machines with. There are many data scientists who argue that the cleaning of data constitutes at least eighty percent of the job. Therefore, if you want to switch to this field, if you are stepping into this field, you must learn how to deal with missing data, messy data, inconsistent formatting, outliers and malformed records.

In this chapter, we will look at how to use the NumPy and Pandas libraries to clean the data sets. We will look at the following points:

- How to drop columns in a DataFrame

- How to change the index in a DataFrame

- How to clean the columns using .str()

- How to use the functioning DataFrame.applymap() to clean the complete data set

- How to rename columns with recognizable labels

- How to skip unnecessary rows

In this chapter, we will be using the following data sets:

- BL-Flickr-Images-Book.csv – This is a csv file which has information about the books in the British Library

- university_towns.txt – This is a text file which contains information about the college towns in the US

- olympics.csv – This is a csv file which provides a summary of the countries that participated in the Summer and Winter Olympics

These data sets can be downloaded from the GitHub repository for Python. Let us first import the NumPy and Pandas libraries to begin with the cleaning of data.

>>>

import pandas as pd

import numpy as np

Dropping Columns In A Data Frame

You will see that you can use most categories of data in the data set for analysis. For instance, you are probably looking at a database that contains student information, including their personal information, but you only want to focus on the analysis of their grades. In this instance, the personal information is not necessary or important for you. You can remove these categories to reduce the amount of space that is taken up by the data set thereby improving the performance of the program.

When you use Pandas, you can remove any unwanted row or column in a DataFrame using the drop() function. Let us now look at an example where we remove columns from a DataFrame. Before we do this, we must create a DataFrame of the BL-Flickr-Images-Book.csv file.

First, let's create a DataFrame out of the CSV file 'BL-Flickr-Images-Book.csv'. In the following example, we will be passing the path to pd.read.csv. This means that all the datasets from the csv file are saved in the folder named Datasets in the current working directory.

>>>

df = pd.read_csv('Datasets/BL-Flickr-Images-Book.csv')

df.head()

Identifier Edition Statement Place of Publication \

0 206 NaN London

1 216 NaN London; Virtue & Yorston

2 218 NaN London

3 472 NaN London

4 480 A new edition, revised, etc. London

Date of Publication Publisher \

0 1879 [1878] S. Tinsley & Co.

1 1868 Virtue & Co.

2 1869 Bradbury, Evans & Co.

3 1851 James Darling

4 1857 Wertheim & Macintosh

Title Author \

0 Walter Forbes. [A novel.] By A. A A. A.

1 All for Greed. [A novel. The dedication signed...
A., A. A.

2 Love the Avenger. By the author of "All for Gr...
A., A. A.

3 Welsh Sketches, chiefly ecclesiastical, to the...
A., E. S.

4 [The World in which I live, and my place in it...
A., E. S.

Contributors Corporate Author \

0 FORBES, Walter. NaN

1 BLAZE DE BURY, Marie Pauline Rose -
Baroness NaN

2 BLAZE DE BURY, Marie Pauline Rose -
Baroness NaN

3 Appleyard, Ernest Silvanus. NaN

4 BROOME, John Henry. NaN

Corporate Contributors Former owner Engraver
Issuance type \

0 NaN NaN NaN monographic

1 NaN NaN NaN monographic

2 NaN NaN NaN monographic

3 NaN NaN NaN monographic

4 NaN NaN NaN monographic

Flickr URL \

http://www.flickr.com/photos/britishlibrary/ta...

1 http://www.flickr.com/photos/britishlibrary/ta...

2 http://www.flickr.com/photos/britishlibrary/ta...

3 http://www.flickr.com/photos/britishlibrary/ta...

4 http://www.flickr.com/photos/britishlibrary/ta...

Shelfmarks

0 British Library HMNTS 12641.b.30.

1 British Library HMNTS 12626.cc.2.

2 British Library HMNTS 12625.dd.1.

3 British Library HMNTS 10369.bbb.15.

4 British Library HMNTS 9007.d.28.

We use the head() method to look at the first five entries. You will see that some of the columns provide some information about the various books which will help the library, but that information is not descriptive about the books: Edition Statement, Corporate Author, Corporate Contributors, Former owner, Engraver, Issuance type and Shelfmarks.

To drop these columns, use the code below:

```
>>>

to_drop = ['Edition Statement',

... 'Corporate Author',

... 'Corporate Contributors',

... 'Former owner',

... 'Engraver',

... 'Contributors',

... 'Issuance type',

... 'Shelfmarks']

df.drop(to_drop, inplace=True, axis=1)
```

In the section above, we have listed the columns that we want to remove from the data set. For this, we will use the drop() function on the object, and pass the axis parameter as one and the inplace parameter as true. This will tell the Pandas directory that you want to change the object directly, and the directory should look for all the values in the column of that object that should be dropped.

When you look at the DataFrame now, you will see that the columns that we do not want to use have been removed.

```
>>>

>>> df.head()
```

Identifier Place of Publication Date of Publication \

0 206 London 1879 [1878]

1 216 London; Virtue & Yorston 1868

2 218 London 1869

3 472 London 1851

4 480 London 1857

Publisher Title \

S. Tinsley & Co. Walter Forbes. [A novel.] By A. A

1 Virtue & Co. All for Greed. [A novel. The dedication signed...

2 Bradbury, Evans & Co. Love the Avenger. By the author of "All for Gr...

3 James Darling Welsh Sketches, chiefly ecclesiastical, to the...

4 Wertheim & Macintosh [The World in which I live, and my place in it...

Author Flickr URL

0 A. A.
http://www.flickr.com/photos/britishlibrary/ta...

1 A., A. A.
http://www.flickr.com/photos/britishlibrary/ta...

2 A., A. A.

http://www.flickr.com/photos/britishlibrary/ta...

3 A., E. S.

http://www.flickr.com/photos/britishlibrary/ta...

4 A., E. S.

http://www.flickr.com/photos/britishlibrary/ta...

You can also choose to remove the columns using the columns parameter instead of specifying which labels the directory needs to look at, and which axis should be considered.

```
>>>
```

```
>>> df.drop(columns=to_drop, inplace=True)
```

This is a readable and a more intuitive syntax. It is apparent what we are doing here. If you know the columns that you want to retain, you can pass them through the argument usecols in the pd.read.csv function.

Changing The Index Of A Data Frame

The Index function in Pandas will allow you to extend the functionality of arrays in the NumPy directories. The function will also allow you to slice and label the data with ease. It is always a good idea to use a unique value to identify a field in the data set. For instance, you can expect that a librarian will always input the unique identifier for every book if he or she needs to search for the record.

>>>

df['Identifier'].is_unique

True

You can use the set_index method to replace the existing index using a column.

df = df.set_index('Identifier')

df.head()

Place of Publication Date of Publication \

206 London 1879 [1878]

216 London; Virtue & Yorston 1868

218 London 1869

472 London 1851

480 London 1857

Publisher \

206 S. Tinsley & Co.

216 Virtue & Co.

218 Bradbury, Evans & Co.

472 James Darling

480 Wertheim & Macintosh

Title Author \

206 Walter Forbes. [A novel.] By A. A A. A.

216 All for Greed. [A novel. The dedication signed... A., A. A.

218 Love the Avenger. By the author of "All for Gr... A., A. A.

472 Welsh Sketches, chiefly ecclesiastical, to the... A., E. S.

480 [The World in which I live, and my place in it... A., E. S.

Flickr URL

http://www.flickr.com/photos/britishlibrary/ta...

http://www.flickr.com/photos/britishlibrary/ta...

http://www.flickr.com/photos/britishlibrary/ta...

http://www.flickr.com/photos/britishlibrary/ta...

http://www.flickr.com/photos/britishlibrary/ta...

Every record in the DataFrame can be accessed using the loc[] function. This function will allow you to give every element in the cell an index based on the label. This means that you can give the record an index regardless of its position.

>>>

```
>>> df.loc[206]
```

Place of Publication London

Date of Publication 1879 [1878]

Publisher S. Tinsley & Co.

Title Walter Forbes. [A novel.] By A. A

Author A. A.

Flickr URL
http://www.flickr.com/photos/britishlibrary/ta...

Name: 206, dtype: object

The number 206 is the first label for all the indices. If you want to access the label using its position, you can use df.iloc[0]. This function will give the element an index based on its position. .loc[] is a class instance, and it has a special syntax which does not follow the rules of a Python instance.

In the previous sections, the index being used was RangeIndex. This function labeled the elements with an index using integers, and this is analogous to the steps performed by the in-built function range. When you pass a column name to the set_index function, you will need to use the values in Identifier to change the index. If you looked closely, you would have noticed that we now use the object returned by the df = df.set_index(...) method as the variable. This is because this method does not make any changes directly to the object, but it does return a modified copy of that object. If you want to avoid this, you should schedule the inplace parameter.

df.set_index('Identifier', inplace=True)

Tidying up Fields in the Data

We have now removed all the unnecessary columns in the DataFrame, and changed the indices to the DataFrame to something that is more sensible. This section will explain to you how you can only work on specific columns, and format them to help you get a better understanding. This will also help you enforce some consistency. We will be cleaning the fields Place of Publication and Date of Publication. When you inspect the data set further, you will notice that every data type is currently dtype. This object is similar to the str type in Python. This data type can encapsulate every field which cannot be labeled as categorical or numerical data. It makes sense to use this since we will be working with data sets that have a bunch of messy strings.

```
>>>
```

```
>>> df.get_dtype_counts()
```

object 6

You can enforce some numeric value to the date of publication field. This will allow you to perform other calculations down the road.

```
>>>
```

```
df.loc[1905:, 'Date of Publication'].head(10)
Identifier
```

1905 1888

1929 1839, 38-54

2836 [1897?]

2854 1865

2956 1860-63

2957 1873

3017 1866

3131 1899

4598 1814

4884 1820

Name: Date of Publication, dtype: object

Every book can only have a single date of publication. Therefore, we will need to do the following:

- The extra dates in the square brackets need to be removed.

- The date ranges should always be converted to the "start date" wherever they are present

- If we are uncertain about some dates, we will need to remove those dates and replace them with NaN from the NumPy directory

- Convert the string nan to the NaN value

You can take advantage of the regular expression by synthesizing these patterns. This will allow you to extract the year of publication.

```
>>>

regex = r'^(\d{4})'
```

You can find the four digits at the start of the string using the above regular expression. This is enough for us. The example used in the section above is a raw string. This means that the backslash used in this string cannot be used as an escape character. This is the standard practice when it comes to regular expressions. (4) in the above string will repeat the rule four times while \d represents a digit. The ^ depicts the start of the string, and the parentheses will denote the capturing group. This will signal to the Pandas directory that we only want to extract a portion of the regular expression. Let us now run this regular expression or regex across the DataFrame.

```
>>>

extr = df['Date of Publication'].str.extract(r'^(\d{4})', expand=False)

extr.head()

Identifier

1879

1868

1869

1851
```

1857

Name: Date of Publication, dtype: object

This column still has dtype, which is a string object. You can obtain the numerical version of that object using the pd.to.numeric function.

```
>>>
```

df['Date of Publication'] = pd.to_numeric(extr)

df['Date of Publication'].dtype dtype('float64')

This will show you that at least one value is missing from ten values, This should not worry you since you can now perform functions on all the valid values in the DataFrame.

```
>>>
```

df['Date of Publication'].isnull().sum() / len(df)
0.11717147339205986

This is now done.

Combining NumPy and Str Methods to Clean Columns

In the above section, you will have noticed that the df['Date of Publication'].str is used to access some string operations in the Pandas directory. This attribute performs functions on compiled regular expressions or Python strings. If you want to clean the Place of Publication field, you will need to combine the str method from the Pandas directories with the np.where function from the NumPy directories. This means that you will be creating a vectorized form of the if loop in Excel. The syntax is as follows:

```
>>>
```

```
>>> np.where(condition, then, else)
```

In the above section, the term condition can hold a Boolean mask or an array-like object. The then value is to be looked at if the condition is true, and the else section is looked at if the condition is false. The .where() method will take every cell or element, and check that element against the condition. If the value of the condition is True, the context in the condition will hold true, while the else condition is run if the condition is False. This can also be nested into a complex if-then statement, which will allow you to compute the values that are based on many conditions.

```
>>>
np.where(condition1, x1, np.where(condition2, x2, np.where(condition3, x3, ...)))
```

Since the Place of Publication column has only string values, we will be using these two functions to clean it. The contents of the column are given below:

```
>>>
df['Place of Publication'].head(10) Identifier

206 London

216 London; Virtue & Yorston

218 London
```

472 London

480 London

481 London

519 London

667 pp. 40. G. Bryan & Co: Oxford, 1898 London]

1143 London

Name: Place of Publication, dtype: object

You will notice that for some rows, there is some unnecessary information which surrounds the place of publication. If you look at the values closely, you will notice that this is only for some rows, especially for those rows where the place of publication is 'Oxford' or 'London.' Let us now look at two different entries:

>>>

>>> df.loc[4157862]

Place of Publication Newcastle-upon-Tyne

Date of Publication 1867

Publisher T. Fordyce

Title Local Records; or, Historical Register of rema...

Author T. Fordyce

Flickr URL
http://www.flickr.com/photos/britishlibrary/ta...

Name: 4157862, dtype: object

```
>>> df.loc[4159587]
```

Place of Publication Newcastle upon Tyne

Date of Publication 1834

Publisher Mackenzie & Dent

Title An historical, topographical and descriptive v...

Author E. (Eneas) Mackenzie

Flickr URL
http://www.flickr.com/photos/britishlibrary/ta...

Name: 4159587, dtype: object

The books in the above list were published at the same time and in the same place, but there is one that has a hyphen while the other does not. You can use the str.contains() function to clean this column in one shot. Use the code below to clean these columns:

```
>>>

pub = df['Place of Publication']

london = pub.str.contains('London')

london[:5]
```

Identifier

True

True

True

True

True

Name: Place of Publication, dtype: bool

>>> oxford = pub.str.contains('Oxford')

These can be combined using the method np.where.

>>>

df['Place of Publication'] = np.where(london, 'London', np.where(oxford, 'Oxford',

pub.str.replace('-', ' ')))

df['Place of Publication'].head() Identifier

206 London

216 London

218 London

472 London

480 London

Name: Place of Publication, dtype: object

In the above example, the np.where() function is

the nested structure. The condition in this structure is a series of Boolean values that are obtained using the function str.contains(). The contains() method allows Python to look for an entity in the substring of a string or an iterable. This method is similar to the in keyword. The replacement that you will need to use is a string that will represent the place of publication. You can also replace a hyphen using a space. This can be done using the str.replace() function, and the column can be reassigned in the DataFrame. It is true that there is a lot more messy data in the DataFrame, but we will look at these columns for now. Let us now look at the first five rows in the DataFrame which looked better than they did when we started,

```
>>>

>>> df.head()
```

Place of Publication Date of Publication Publisher \

206 London 1879 S. Tinsley & Co.

216 London 1868 Virtue & Co.

218 London 1869 Bradbury, Evans & Co.

472 London 1851 James Darling

480 London 1857 Wertheim & Macintosh

Title Author \

206 Walter Forbes. [A novel.] By A. A AA

216 All for Greed. [A novel. The dedication signed... A. A A.

218 Love the Avenger. By the author of "All for Gr... A. A A.

472 Welsh Sketches, chiefly ecclesiastical, to the... E. S A.

480 [The World in which I live, and my place in it... E. S A.

Flickr URL

http://www.flickr.com/photos/britishlibrary/ta...

http://www.flickr.com/photos/britishlibrary/ta...

http://www.flickr.com/photos/britishlibrary/ta...

http://www.flickr.com/photos/britishlibrary/ta...

http://www.flickr.com/photos/britishlibrary/ta...

Cleaning the Entire Dataset Using the applymap()

In some instances, you will see that the "mess" is not only in one column, but can be found across the data set. You may need to apply a function to every cell or element in the data frame in some instances. You can use the applymap() function to apply one function to every cell or element in the DataFrame. This function is similar to the map() function. Let us look at the following example where we will create a DataFrame using the university_towns.txt file.

head Datasets/univerisity_towns.txt
Alabama[edit]

Auburn (Auburn University)[1] Florence

(University of North Alabama) Jacksonville (Jacksonville State University)[2] Livingston (University of West Alabama)[2] Montevallo (University of Montevallo)[2] Troy (Troy University)[2]

Tuscaloosa (University of Alabama, Stillman College, Shelton State)[3][4] Tuskegee (Tuskegee University)[5]

Alaska[edit]

In the above section, you will see that there every periodic state name is followed by a university town in that state. For example, StateA TownA1 TownA2. If you look at how the names of the states are written, you will see that each one of them has the "[edit]" substring, You can create a list of tuples in the form (State, City), and wrap that list using a DataFrame.

>>>

university_towns = []

with   open('Datasets/university_towns.txt')   as

file:

... for line in file:

... if '[edit]' in line:

... # Remember this `state` until the next is found

... state = line

... else:

... # Otherwise, we have a city; keep `state` as last-seen

... university_towns.append((state, line))

university_towns[:5]

[('Alabama[edit]\n', 'Auburn (Auburn University)[1]\n'), ('Alabama[edit]\n', 'Florence (University of North Alabama)\n'), ('Alabama[edit]\n', 'Jacksonville (Jacksonville State University)[2]\n'), ('Alabama[edit]\n', 'Livingston (University of West Alabama)[2]\n'), ('Alabama[edit]\n', 'Montevallo (University of

Montevallo)[2]\n')]

This list can be wrapped using a DataFrame, and the columns can be set to "RegionName" and "State." The Pandas directory will consider every element in the above list and set the left value to State and the right value to RegionName. The DataFrame will now look like this:

>>>

towns_df = pd.DataFrame(university_towns,

... columns=['State', 'RegionName'])

towns_df.head()

State RegionName

0   Alabama[edit]\n   Auburn   (Auburn University)[1]\n

1 Alabama[edit]\n Florence (University of North Alabama)\n

2 Alabama[edit]\n Jacksonville (Jacksonville State University)[2]\n

3 Alabama[edit]\n Livingston (University of West Alabama)[2]\n

4 Alabama[edit]\n Montevallo (University of Montevallo)[2]\n

The strings could have been fixed or cleaned in the loop above. The Pandas directory will make it easier for you to do this. All you need is the name of the town and the state, and you can remove everything else. We can use the .str() method in this instance, but you can also use the applymap() method to map every element in the DataFrame to a Python callable. To understand what we mean by the term "element," you must look at the example given below:

>>>

1

Mock Dataset

1 Python Pandas

2 Real Python

3 NumPy Clean

In the above example, every cell is considered an element. Therefore, the applymap() function will look at each of these cells independently, and apply the necessary function. Let us now define that function:

>>>

def get_citystate(item):

... if ' (' in item:

... return item[:item.find(' (')]

... elif '[' in item:

... return item[:item.find('[')]

... else:

... return item

The applymap() function in the Pandas directory only takes one parameter. This parameter is the function, also called the callable, which can be applied to every element.

>>>

```
>>> towns_df =
towns_df.applymap(get_citystate)
```

We will first need to define a function in Python which will pick an element as a parameter from the DataFrame. A check will then be performed within the function to determine whether the element contains a "(" or "[" or not. Based on the value of the check, the values are mapped to that element by the function. The applymap() function will then be called on the object. If you look at the DataFrame now, you will see that it is neater than before.

```
>>>
```

towns_df.head() State RegionName

0 Alabama Auburn

1 Alabama Florence

2 Alabama Jacksonville

3 Alabama Livingston

4 Alabama Montevallo

In the above section of the code, the applymap() method looked at every element in the DataFrame, and passed that element to the function after which the returned value was used to replace the original value. It is this simple. The applymap() method is both a convenient and versatile method. This method can, however, take some time to run for large data sets. This is because it maps every individual element to a Python callable. Therefore, it is always a good idea to use vectorized operations that use the NumPy or Cython directories.

Renaming Columns and Skipping Rows

There are times when you will have datasets that have some unnecessary or unimportant information in the first or last rows or column names that are difficult to understand. For instance, there can be some definitions or some footnotes in the data set which are not necessary for you to use. In this case, you should skip those rows or rename the columns, so you can remove the unnecessary information or work with sensible labels. Let us first look at the first few rows in the Olympics.csv data set before we look at how this can be done.

head -n 5 Datasets/olympics.csv

0,1,2,3,4,5,6,7,8,9,10,11,12,13,14,15

,? Summer,01 !,02 !,03 !,Total,? Winter,01 !,02 !,03 !,Total,? Games,01 !,02 !,03 !,Combined total

Afghanistan (AFG),13,0,0,2,2,0,0,0,0,0,13,0,0,2,2

Algeria (ALG),12,5,2,8,15,3,0,0,0,0,15,5,2,8,15

Argentina (ARG),23,18,24,28,70,18,0,0,0,0,41,18,24,28,70

Now, we'll read it into a Pandas DataFrame:

>>>

>>> olympics_df = pd.read_csv('Datasets/olympics.csv')

```
>>> olympics_df.head()
```

0 1 2 3 4 5 6 7 8 \

0 NaN ? Summer 01 ! 02 ! 03 ! Total ? Winter 01 !
02 ! 1 Afghanistan (AFG) 13 0 0 2 2 0 0 0

2 Algeria (ALG) 12 5 2 8 15 3 0 0

3 Argentina (ARG) 23 18 24 28 70 18 0 0 4
Armenia (ARM) 5 1 2 9 12 6 0 0

9 10 11 12 13 14 15

0 03 ! Total ? Games 01 ! 02 ! 03 ! Combined
total

1 0 0 13 0 0 2 2

2 0 0 15 5 2 8 15

3 0 0 41 18 24 28 70

4 0 0 11 1 2 9 12

This is certainly messy. Every column is indexed
at zero, and is the string form of the integer. The
row that you are using to set the names of the

other columns is at the Olympics_df.iloc[0]. This is because the file that we are using starts the indexing at 0 and ends at 15.

If you want to go to the source of the dataset, you will see that Nan above a column will represent Country, "? Summer" will represent the Summer Games, "01!" represents Gold, etc. Therefore, we will need to do the following:

Skip the first row and set the index as zero for the headers Rename all the columns

You can pass some parameters in the read.csv() function if you want to skip some rows and set the index for the headers as one. The function read.csv does use a lot of parameters, but in this instance, we only need to remove the first row (which has the index zero).

>>> olympics_df = pd.read_csv('Datasets/olympics.csv', header=1)

olympics_df.head()

Unnamed: 0 ? Summer 01 ! 02 ! 03 ! Total ?

Winter \ 0 Afghanistan (AFG) 13 0 0 2 2 0 1
Algeria (ALG) 12 5 2 8 15 3

2 Argentina (ARG) 23 18 24 28 70 18

3 Armenia (ARM) 5 1 2 9 12 6

4 Australasia (ANZ) [ANZ] 2 3 4 5 12 0

01 !.1 02 !.1 03 !.1 Total.1 ? Games 01 !.2 02 !.2 03 !.2 \

0 0 0 0 0 13 0 0 2

1 0 0 0 0 15 5 2 8

2 0 0 0 0 41 18 24 28

3 0 0 0 0 11 1 2 9

4 0 0 0 0 2 3 4 5

Combined total

2

1 15

2 70

3 12

4 12

The dataset no longer has any unnecessary rows, and the correct names have been used for all fields. You should see how the Pandas library has changed the name of the Countries column from NaN to Unnamed: 0.

To rename the columns, we will use the rename() method in the DataFrame. This will allow you to re-label any axis in the data set using a mapping. In this instance, we will need to use dict. We must first define the dictionary which will map the existing names of the columns to the usable names which are present in the dictionary.

>>>

new_names = {'Unnamed: 0': 'Country',

... '? Summer': 'Summer Olympics',

... '01 !': 'Gold',

... '02 !': 'Silver',

... '03 !': 'Bronze',

... '? Winter': 'Winter Olympics',

... '01 !.1': 'Gold.1',

... '02 !.1': 'Silver.1',

... '03 !.1': 'Bronze.1',

... '? Games': '# Games',

... '01 !.2': 'Gold.2',

... '02 !.2': 'Silver.2',

... '03 !.2': 'Bronze.2'}

We will now call upon the rename() function on the object.

```
>>>

>>> olympics_df.rename(columns=new_names, inplace=True)
```

If you want changes to be made directly to the object, you should set inplace to true. Let us see if this works for us:

```
>>>

>>> olympics_df.head()
```

Country Summer Olympics Gold Silver Bronze

Total \

0 Afghanistan (AFG) 13 0 0 2 2

1 Algeria (ALG) 12 5 2 8 15

2 Argentina (ARG) 23 18 24 28 70

3 Armenia (ARM) 5 1 2 9 12

4 Australasia (ANZ) [ANZ] 2 3 4 5 12

Winter Olympics Gold.1 Silver.1 Bronze.1 Total.1
Games Gold.2 \

0 0 0 0 0 0 13 0

1 3 0 0 0 0 15 5

2 18 0 0 0 0 41 18

3 6 0 0 0 0 11 1

4 0 0 0 0 0 2 3

Silver.2 Bronze.2 Combined total

0 0 2 2

1 2 8 15

2 24 28 70

3 2 9 12

4 4 5 12

Python Data Cleaning: Recap and Resources

In this chapter, you gathered information on how you can remove any unnecessary fields in a dataset, and how you can set an index for every field in the dataset to make it easier for you to access that field. You also learnt how you can use the applymap() function to clean the complete dataset, and to use the .str() accessor to clean specific object fields. It is important to know how to clean data since it is a big part of data analytics. You now know how you can use NumPy and Pandas to clean different data sets.

Chapter Nine: How to Manipulate Data Using Python

In this chapter, we will learn more about how we can use the NumPy and Pandas libraries to manipulate the data.

Starting with Numpy

#load the library and check its version, just to make sure we aren't using an older version

import numpy as np

np.__version__

'1.12.1'

#create a list comprising numbers from 0 to 9

L=list(range(10))

#converting integers to string - this style of

handling lists is known as list comprehension.

#List comprehension offers a versatile way to handle list manipulations tasks easily. We'll learn about them in future tutorials. Here's an example.

[str(c) for c in L]

['0', '1', '2', '3', '4', '5', '6', '7', '8', '9']

[type(item) for item in L]

[int, int, int, int, int, int, int, int, int, int]

Creating Arrays

Arrays created in NumPy are always homogeneous in nature. This means that they can only hold variables of the same data type.

#creating arrays

np.zeros(10, dtype='int')

array([0, 0, 0, 0, 0, 0, 0, 0, 0, 0])

```
#creating a 3 row x 5 column matrix

np.ones((3,5), dtype=float)

array([[ 1., 1., 1., 1., 1.],

1., 1., 1., 1., 1.],

1., 1., 1., 1., 1.]])

#creating a matrix with a predefined value
np.full((3,5),1.23)

array([[ 1.23, 1.23, 1.23, 1.23, 1.23],

1.23, 1.23, 1.23, 1.23, 1.23],

1.23, 1.23, 1.23, 1.23, 1.23]]) #create an array with
a set sequence np.arange(0, 20, 2)

array([0, 2, 4, 6, 8,10,12,14,16,18])

#create an array of even space between the given
range of values np.linspace(0, 1, 5)

array([ 0., 0.25, 0.5 , 0.75, 1.])

#create a 3x3 array with mean 0 and standard
deviation 1 in a given dimension
```

```
np.random.normal(0, 1, (3,3))

array([[ 0.72432142, -0.90024075, 0.27363808],
0.88426129,     1.45096856,    -1.03547109],    [-
0.42930994,      -1.02284441,       -1.59753603]])
#create an identity matrix

np.eye(3) array([[ 1., 0., 0.],

0., 1., 0.],

0., 0., 1.]])

#set a random seed np.random.seed(0)

x1   =   np.random.randint(10,   size=6)   #one
dimension

x2  =  np.random.randint(10,  size=(3,4))  #two
dimension

x3 = np.random.randint(10, size=(3,4,5)) #three
dimension

print("x3 ndim:", x3.ndim)

print("x3 shape:", x3.shape)
```

```
print("x3 size: ", x3.size)
```

('x3 ndim:', 3)

('x3 shape:', (3, 4, 5))

('x3 size: ', 60)

Array Indexing

You must remember that indexing in python always begins at zero.

```
x1 = np.array([4, 3, 4, 4, 8, 4])
```

```
x1
```

array([4, 3, 4, 4, 8, 4])

```
#assess value to index zero
```

```
x1[0]
```

4

```
#assess fifth value
```

```
x1[4]
```

8

#get the last value

x1[-1]

4

#get the second last value

x1[-2]

8

#in a multidimensional array, we need to specify row and column index x2

array([[3, 7, 5, 5],

[0, 1, 5, 9],

[3, 0, 5, 0]])

#1st row and 2nd column value

x2[2,3]

0

#3rd row and last value from the 3rd column

```
x2[2,-1]
```

```
0
```

```
#replace value at 0,0 index
```

```
x2[0,0] = 12
```

```
x2
```

```
array([[12, 7, 5, 5],

0, 1, 5, 9],

3, 0, 5, 0]])
```

Array Slicing

Let us now see how we can access a range of elements or multiple elements in an array.

```
x = np.arange(10)
```

```
x
```

```
array([0, 1, 2, 3, 4, 5, 6, 7, 8, 9])
```

```
#from start to 4th position
```

```
x[:5]
```

```
array([0, 1, 2, 3, 4])

#from 4th position to end

x[4:]

array([4, 5, 6, 7, 8, 9])

#from 4th to 6th position

x[4:7]

array([4, 5, 6])

#return elements at even place

x[ : : 2]

array([0, 2, 4, 6, 8])

#return elements from first position step by two

x[1::2]

array([1, 3, 5, 7, 9])

#reverse the array

x[::-1]

array([9, 8, 7, 6, 5, 4, 3, 2, 1, 0])
```

Array Concatenation

There will be times when you will need to combine multiple arrays. Instead of typing the elements manually, you can concatenate them to make it easier to handle such tasks.

#You can concatenate two or more arrays at once.

x = np.array([1, 2, 3])

y = np.array([3, 2, 1])

z = [21,21,21]

np.concatenate([x, y,z])

array([1, 2, 3, 3, 2, 1, 21, 21, 21])

#You can also use this function to create 2-dimensional arrays.

grid = np.array([[1,2,3],[4,5,6]])

np.concatenate([grid,grid])

```
array([[1, 2, 3],

[4, 5, 6],

[1, 2, 3],

[4, 5, 6]])
```

#Using its axis parameter, you can define row-wise or column-wise matrix

```
np.concatenate([grid,grid],axis=1)

array([[1, 2, 3, 1, 2, 3],

[4, 5, 6, 4, 5, 6]])
```

We have only used the concatenation function until now on arrays that have the same dimension. So, what should you do if you want to combine a one-dimensional array with a two-dimensional array? You should use the np.hstack or np.vstack in such instances. Let us look at how this can be done.

```
x = np.array([3,4,5])

grid = np.array([[1,2,3],[17,18,19]])
```

```
np.vstack([x,grid])

array([[ 3, 4, 5],

1, 2, 3], [17, 18, 19]])

#Similarly, you can add an array using np.hstack
z = np.array([[9],[9]])

np.hstack([grid,z]) array([[ 1, 2, 3, 9], [17, 18, 19, 9]])
```

You can use some pre-defined conditions or positions to split the array. x = np.arange(10)

```
x

array([0, 1, 2, 3, 4, 5, 6, 7, 8, 9]) x1,x2,x3 = np.split(x,[3,6]) print x1,x2,x3

[0 1 2] [3 4 5] [6 7 8 9]

grid = np.arange(16).reshape((4,4)) grid

upper,lower = np.vsplit(grid,[2]) print (upper, lower)

(array([[0, 1, 2, 3],
```

[4, 5, 6, 7]]), array([[8, 9, 10, 11], [12, 13, 14, 15]]))

There are many mathematical functions, apart from the functions used above, in the NumPy directories that you can use. Some examples are sum, divide, abs, multiple, mod, power, log, sin, tan, cos, mean, min, max, var, etc. These functions can be used to perform some arithmetic calculations. You should refer to the NumPy documentation to learn more about these functions. Let us now look at the Pandas directories. You must ensure that you read every line carefully to ensure that you perform data manipulation well.

Let's start with Pandas

#load library - pd is just an alias. I used pd because it's short and literally abbreviates pandas.

#You can use any name as an alias.

```python
import pandas as pd
```

#create a data frame - dictionary is used here where keys get converted to column names and values to row values.

```python
data = pd.DataFrame({'Country':
['Russia','Colombia','Chile','Equador','Nigeria'],

Rank':[121,40,100,130,11]})
```

```python
data
```

CountryRank

0Russia121

1Colombia40

2Chile100

3Equador130

4Nigeria11

#We can do a quick analysis of any data set using:

```python
data.describe()
```

Rank

count5.000000

mean80.400000

std52.300096

min11.000000

25%40.000000

50%100.000000

75%121.000000

max130.000000

You must remember that the method describe() will give you the summary statistics of the integer or double variables alone. If you want to obtain the complete information about the data set, you should use the info() function.

#Among other things, it shows the data set has 5 rows and 2 columns with their respective names.
data.info()

```
<class 'pandas.core.frame.DataFrame'>

RangeIndex: 5 entries, 0 to 4

Data columns (total 2 columns):

Country 5 non-null object

Rank 5 non-null int64

dtypes: int64(1), object(1)

memory usage: 152.0+ bytes

#Let's create another data frame.

data = pd.DataFrame({'group':['a', 'a', 'a', 'b','b',
'b', 'c', 'c','c'],'ounces':[4, 3, 12, 6, 7.5, 8, 3, 5, 6]})

data

groupounces

0a4.0

1a3.0

2a12.0

3b6.0
```

4b7.5

5b8.0

6c3.0

7c5.0

8c6.0

#Let's sort the data frame by ounces - inplace = True will make changes to the data data.sort_values(by=['ounces'],ascending=True,inplace=False) groupounces

1a3.0

6c3.0

0a4.0

7c5.0

3b6.0

8c6.0

4b7.5

5b8.0

2a12.0

You can now sort the data using multiple columns.

data.sort_values(by=['group','ounces'],ascending
=[True,False],inplace=False)

groupounces

2a12.0

0a4.0

1a3.0

5b8.0

4b7.5

3b6.0

8c6.0

7c5.0

6c3.0

We often get a data set that has duplicate rows, and these rows are only noise. It is for this reason that you must remove any such inconsistencies in the data set before you train the model. Let us now see how we can remove the duplicate rows.

```
#create another data with duplicated rows

data = pd.DataFrame({'k1':['one']*3 + ['two']*4,
'k2':[3,2,1,3,3,4,4]})

data
```

k1k2

0one3

1one2

2one1

3two3

4two3

5two4

6two4

```
#sort values

data.sort_values(by='k2')
```

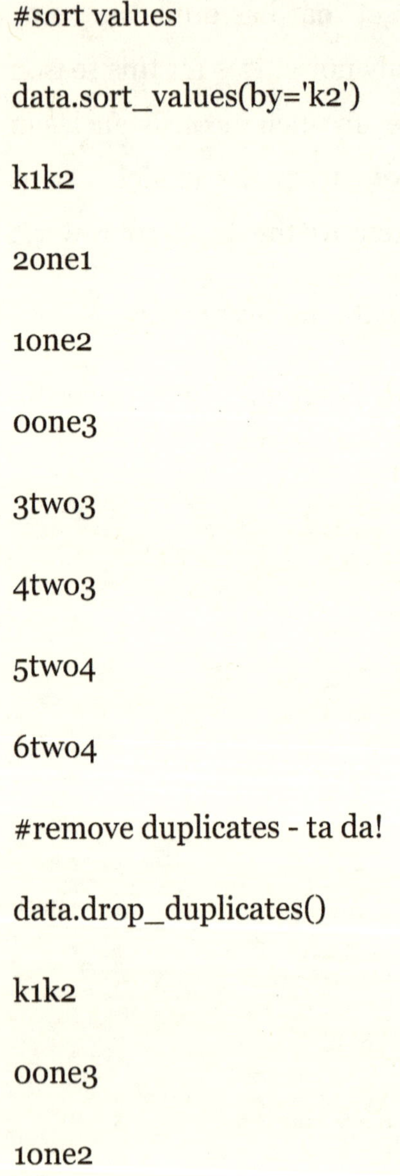

```
k1k2

2one1

1one2

0one3

3two3

4two3

5two4

6two4
```

```
#remove duplicates - ta da!

data.drop_duplicates()
```

```
k1k2

0one3

1one2
```

2one1

3two3

5two4

In the above example, we have matched the values in the rows across all the column to remove any duplicates. You can also remove any duplicates based on specific columns. Let us now remove all the duplicate values in the Column K1.

data.drop_duplicates(subset='k1')

k1k2

0one3

3two3

Let us now learn how we can categorize the rows using some predefined criteria. This will happen quite a bit when you process data, especially that data where you will need to categorize some variables. For instance, let us assume that you have a column that has the names of all the countries in it. You want to place those countries into their respective continents, and because of this you will need to create a new variable. For this, you will need to follow the steps given below:

data = pd.DataFrame({'food': ['bacon', 'pulled pork', 'bacon', 'Pastrami','corned beef', 'Bacon', 'pastrami', 'honey ham','nova lox'],

'ounces': [4, 3, 12, 6, 7.5, 8, 3, 5, 6]})

data

foodounces

0bacon4.0

1pulled pork3.0

2bacon12.0

3Pastrami6.0

4corned beef7.5

5Bacon8.0

6pastrami3.0

7honey ham5.0

8nova lox6.0

We will now create some new variables that will indicate what type of animal will act the source of food for another. For this, we will first need to map the food to the animals using the dictionary. We can then use the map function to map the values in the dictionary to the keys. Let us look at how this can be done.

```
meat_to_animal = {

'bacon': 'pig',

'pulled pork': 'pig',

'pastrami': 'cow',

'corned beef': 'cow',

'honey ham': 'pig',

'nova lox': 'salmon'

}
```

```python
def meat_2_animal(series):

    if series['food'] == 'bacon':

        return 'pig'

    elif series['food'] == 'pulled pork':

        return 'pig'

    elif series['food'] == 'pastrami':

        return 'cow'

    elif series['food'] == 'corned beef':

        return 'cow'

    elif series['food'] == 'honey ham':

        return 'pig'

    else:

        return 'salmon'

#create a new variable
data['animal']                                    =
data['food'].map(str.lower).map(meat_to_anima
```

```
l)

data

         food  ounces  animal
0        bacon     4.0    pig
1  pulled pork     3.0    pig
2        bacon    12.0    pig
3     Pastrami     6.0    cow
4  corned beef     7.5    cow
5        Bacon     8.0    pig
6     pastrami     3.0    cow
7    honey ham     5.0    pig
8     nova lox     6.0 salmon
```

#another way of doing it is: convert the food values to the lower case and apply the function

```
lower = lambda x: x.lower()

data['food'] = data['food'].apply(lower)
```

```
data['animal2']    =    data.apply(meat_2_animal,
axis='columns')

data
```

foodouncesanimalanimal2

0bacon4.0pigpig

1pulled pork3.0pigpig

2bacon12.0pigpig

3pastrami6.0cowcow

4corned beef7.5cowcow

5bacon8.0pigpig

6pastrami3.0cowcow

7honey ham5.0pigpig

8nova lox6.0salmonsalmon

You can use the assign function to create another variable. This chapter will teach you some new functions which you will need to keep in mind. You will also realize why it is important to understand the Pandas directory well.

```
data.assign(new_variable = data['ounces']*10)
```

foodouncesanimalanimal2new_variable

0bacon4.0pigpig40.0

1pulled pork3.0pigpig30.0

2bacon12.0pigpig120.0

3pastrami6.0cowcow60.0

4corned beef7.5cowcow75.0

5bacon8.0pigpig80.0

6pastrami3.0cowcow30.0

7honey ham5.0pigpig50.0

8nova lox6.0salmonsalmon60.0

Let us now remove the animal2 column from the data frame.

```
data.drop('animal2',axis='columns',inplace=True
)
```

data

foodouncesanimal

0bacon4.0pig

1pulled pork3.0pig

2bacon12.0pig

3Pastrami6.0cow

4corned beef7.5cow

5Bacon8.0pig

6pastrami3.0cow

7honey ham5.0pig

8nova lox6.0salmon

There are times when you will find some missing values in the data set. You can choose to input a missing value in the data set with any random number. There is a probability of there being outliers in the data set, and you can use some dummy or default values as a substitute to those values. Let us see how we can replace these values in the data set.

```
#Series function from pandas are used to create arrays

data = pd.Series([1., -999., 2., -999., -1000., 3.])

data
```

0 1.0

-999.0

2 2.0

3 -999.0

4 -1000.0

5 3.0

dtype: float64

```
#replace -999 with NaN values data.replace(-999, np.nan,inplace=True) data
```

0 1.0

NaN

2.0

3 NaN

4 -1000.0

5 3.0

dtype: float64

```
#We can also replace multiple values at once.
data = pd.Series([1., -999., 2., -999., -1000., 3.])
data.replace([-999,-1000],np.nan,inplace=True)
data
```

0 1.0

1 NaN

2.0

NaN

4 NaN

5 3.0

dtype: float64

Let us now look at how we can rename the rows and columns.

```
data = pd.DataFrame(np.arange(12).reshape((3, 4)),index=['Ohio', 'Colorado', 'New York'],columns=['one', 'two', 'three', 'four'])

data
```

onetwothreefour

Ohio0123

Colorado4567

New York891011

Using rename function

```
data.rename(index = {'Ohio':'SanF'}, columns={'one':'one_p','two':'two_p'},inplace=True) data
```

one_ptwo_pthreefour

SanF0123

Colorado4567

New York891011

#You can also use string functions

data.rename(index = str.upper, columns=str.title,inplace=True)

data

One_pTwo_pThreeFour

SANF0123

COLORADO4567

NEW YORK891011

We will need to split or categorize the continuous variables.

ages = [20, 22, 25, 27, 21, 23, 37, 31, 61, 45, 41, 32]

Let us now divide the ages into smaller segments or bins like 18-25, 26-35,36-60 and 60 and above.

#Understand the output - '(' means the value is included in the bin, '[' means the value is excluded

bins = [18, 25, 35, 60, 100]

cats = pd.cut(ages, bins)

cats

[(18, 25], (18, 25], (18, 25], (25, 35], (18, 25], ..., (25, 35], (60, 100], (35, 60], (35, 60], (25, 35]]
Length: 12

Categories (4, object): [(18, 25] < (25, 35] < (35, 60] < (60, 100]] #To include the right bin value, we can do: pd.cut(ages,bins,right=False)

[[18, 25), [18, 25), [25, 35), [25, 35), [18, 25), ..., [25, 35), [60, 100), [35, 60), [35, 60), [25, 35)]
Length: 12

Categories (4, object): [[18, 25) < [25, 35) < [35, 60) < [60, 100)] #pandas library intrinsically assigns an encoding to categorical variables. cats.labels array([0, 0, 0, 1, 0, 0, 2, 1, 3, 2, 2, 1], dtype=int8)

#Let's check how many observations fall under each bin

pd.value_counts(cats)

(18, 25] 5

(35, 60] 3

(25, 35] 3

(60, 100] 1

dtype: int64

We can also pass a name to every label.

bin_names = ['Youth', 'YoungAdult', 'MiddleAge', 'Senior']   new_cats   =   pd.cut(ages, bins,labels=bin_names)

pd.value_counts(new_cats)

Youth5

MiddleAge3

YoungAdult3

Senior1

dtype: int64

#we can also calculate their cumulative sum

pd.value_counts(new_cats).cumsum()

Youth5

MiddleAge3

YoungAdult3

Senior1

dtype: int64

Let us now learn more about how we can group data and create pivots using the Pandas directories. It is important to learn how to create a pivot table since it is one of the easiest analysis methods that you can use on any data set that you work with.

df = pd.DataFrame({'key1' : ['a', 'a', 'b', 'b', 'a'],

```python
'key2' : ['one', 'two', 'one', 'two', 'one'],

'data1' : np.random.randn(5),

'data2' : np.random.randn(5)})

df
```

data1data2key1key2

00.9735990.001761a

10.207283-0.990160a

21.0996421.872394b

30.939897-0.241074b

40.6063890.053345a

```python
#calculate the mean of data1 column by key1

grouped = df['data1'].groupby(df['key1'])

grouped.mean()
```

key1

0.595757 b 1.019769

Name: data1, dtype: float64

Now, let's see how to slice the data frame. dates = pd.date_range('20130101',periods=6)

df = pd.DataFrame(np.random.randn(6,4),index=dates,columns=list('ABCD')) df

ABCD

2013-01-011.030816-1.2769890.837720-1.490111

2013-01-02-1.070215-0.2091290.604572-1.743058

2013-01-031.5242271.8635751.2913781.300696

2013-01-040.918203-0.158800-0.964063-1.990779

2013-01-050.0897310.114854-0.5858150.298772

2013-01-060.2222600.435183-0.0457480.049898 #get first n rows from the data frame df[:3]

ABCD

2013-01-011.030816-1.2769890.837720-1.490111

2013-01-02-1.070215-0.2091290.604572-1.743058

2013-01-031.5242271.8635751.2913781.300696

```
#slice based on date range
df['20130101':'20130104']
```

ABCD

2013-01-011.030816-1.2769890.837720-1.490111

2013-01-02-1.070215-0.2091290.604572-1.743058

2013-01-031.5242271.8635751.2913781.300696

2013-01-040.918203-0.158800-0.964063-1.990779

```
#slicing based on column names
df.loc[:,['A','B']]
```

AB

2013-01-011.030816-1.276989

2013-01-02-1.070215-0.209129

2013-01-031.5242271.863575

2013-01-040.918203-0.158800

2013-01-050.0897310.114854

2013-01-060.2222600.435183

#slicing based on both row index labels and column names
df.loc['20130102':'20130103',['A','B']] AB

2013-01-02-1.070215-0.209129

2013-01-031.5242271.863575

#slicing based on index of columns

df.iloc[3] #returns 4th row (index is 3rd)

0.918203 B -0.158800 C -0.964063 D -1.990779

Name: 2013-01-04 00:00:00, dtype: float64
#returns a specific range of rows df.iloc[2:4, 0:2]

AB

2013-01-031.5242271.863575

2013-01-040.918203-0.158800

#returns specific rows and columns using lists containing columns or row indexes

df.iloc[[1,5],[0,2]]

AC

2013-01-02-1.0702150.604572

2013-01-060.222260-0.045748

You can also perform Boolean indexing using the values in the columns. This will help you filter the data set based on some conditions. These conditions must be pre-defined.

df[df.A > 1]

ABCD

2013-01-011.030816-1.2769890.837720-1.490111

2013-01-031.5242271.8635751.2913781.300696

```python
#we can copy the data set

df2 = df.copy()

df2['E']=['one', 'one','two','three','four','three']

df2
```

ABCDE

2013-01-011.030816-1.2769890.837720-1.490111one

2013-01-02-1.070215-0.2091290.604572-1.743058one

2013-01-031.5242271.8635751.2913781.300696two

2013-01-040.918203-0.158800-0.964063-1.990779three

2013-01-050.0897310.114854-0.5858150.298772four

2013-01-060.2222600.435183-0.0457480.049898three #select rows based on column values df2[df2['E'].isin(['two','four'])]

ABCDE

2013-01-031.5242271.8635751.2913781.300696two

2013-01-050.0897310.114854-0.5858150.298772four #select all rows except those with two and four df2[~df2['E'].isin(['two','four'])] ABCDE

2013-01-011.030816-1.2769890.837720-1.490111one

2013-01-02-1.070215-0.2091290.604572-1.743058one

2013-01-040.918203-0.158800-0.964063-1.990779three

2013-01-060.2222600.435183-0.0457480.049898three

You can also select columns using a query method. In this method, you will need to enter a criterion.

#list all columns where A is greater than C

```
df.query('A > C')
```

ABCD

2013-01-011.030816-1.2769890.837720-1.490111

2013-01-031.5242271.8635751.2913781.300696

2013-01-040.918203-0.158800-0.964063-1.990779

2013-01-050.0897310.114854-0.5858150.298772

2013-01-060.2222600.435183-0.0457480.049898

```
#using OR condition
df.query('A < B | C > A')
```

ABCD

2013-01-02-1.070215-0.2091290.604572-1.743058

2013-01-031.5242271.8635751.2913781.300696

2013-01-050.0897310.114854-0.5858150.298772

2013-01-060.2222600.435183-
0.0457480.049898

A pivot table is useful if you want to understand the data set better because you customize the format. Excel is a tool that is used popularly since it easier for people to use a pivot table. This table allows users to analyze data quickly.

```
#create a data frame
data = pd.DataFrame({'group': ['a', 'a', 'a', 'b','b',
'b', 'c', 'c','c'],

'ounces': [4, 3, 12, 6, 7.5, 8, 3, 5, 6]})

data
```

groupounces

0a4.0

1a3.0

2a12.0

3b6.0

```
4b7.5

5b8.0

6c3.0

7c5.0

8c6.0
```

#calculate means of each group

```
data.pivot_table(values='ounces',index='group',aggfunc=np.mean)

group
```

6.333333 b 7.166667 c 4.666667

Name: ounces, dtype: float64 #calculate count by each group

```
data.pivot_table(values='ounces',index='group',aggfunc='count') group
```

3

3 c 3

Name: ounces, dtype: int64

We have now become familiar with the basics of the Pandas library using the example above. We should now look at a real-life data set and see how we can use the information that we have gathered in this chapter to explore that data set.

Exploring ML Data Set[1]

In this section, we will be working with an adult data set that we have taken from the UCI Machine Learning Repository. This data set can be downloaded from the following location: https://s3-ap-southeast-1.amazonaws.com/he-public-data/datafiles19cdaf8.zip.

The dependent variable in this data set is "target." The data set poses a binary classification problem, and we need to predict if the salary of an individual is greater than or less than 50k.

#load the data

---

[1] S3-ap-southeast-1.amazonaws.com. (2019). [online] Available at: https://s3-ap-southeast-1.amazonaws.com/he-public-data/datafiles19cdaf8.zip [Accessed 23 Mar. 2019]

```python
train = pd.read_csv("~/Adult/train.csv")

test = pd.read_csv("~/Adult/test.csv")

#check data set

train.info()
```

<class 'pandas.core.frame.DataFrame'>

RangeIndex: 32561 entries, 0 to 32560

Data columns (total 15 columns):

age 32561 non-null int64

workclass 30725 non-null object

fnlwgt 32561 non-null int64

education 32561 non-null object

education.num 32561 non-null int64

marital.status 32561 non-null object

occupation 30718 non-null object

relationship 32561 non-null object

race 32561 non-null object

sex 32561 non-null object

capital.gain 32561 non-null int64

capital.loss 32561 non-null int64

hours.per.week 32561 non-null int64

native.country 31978 non-null object

target 32561 non-null object

dtypes: int64(6), object(9)

memory usage: 3.7+ MB

This training data set has 15 columns and 32561 rows. There are only six integer classes out of the fifteen columns in the data set. The remaining columns have character or object classes. Similarly, we can check the test data set. You can also look for the number of rows and columns in the following way:

print ("The train data has",train.shape)

```
print ("The test data has",test.shape)
```

('The train data has', (32561, 15))

('The test data has', (16281, 15))

```
#Let have a glimpse of the data set
```

```
train.head()
```

ageworkclassfnlwgteducationeducation.nummari tal.statusoccupationrelationshipracesexcapital.ga incapit

al.losshours.per.weeknative.countrytarget

039State-gov77516Bachelors13Never-marriedAdm-clericalNot-in-familyWhiteMale2174040United-States<=50K

150Self-emp-not-inc83311Bachelors13Married-civ-spouseExec-managerialHusbandWhiteMale0013United-States<=50K

238Private215646HS-grad9DivorcedHandlers-cleanersNot-in-familyWhiteMale0040United-

States<=50K

353Private23472111th7Married-civ-spouseHandlers-cleanersHusbandBlackMale0040United-States<=50K

428Private338409Bachelors13Married-civ-spouseProf-specialtyWifeBlackFemale0040Cuba<=50K   Let us verify if the data set has any missing values.
nans = train.shape[0] - train.dropna().shape[0]

print ("%d rows have missing values in the train data" %nans)

nand = test.shape[0] - test.dropna().shape[0]

print ("%d rows have missing values in the test data" %nand) 2399 rows have missing values in the train data 1221 rows have missing values in the test data

We should now look for those columns that have any missing values.

```python
#only 3 columns have missing values

train.isnull().sum()
```

```
age0

workclass1836

fnlwgt0

education0

education.num0

marital.status0

occupation1843

relationship0

race0

sex0

capital.gain0

capital.loss0

hours.per.week0
```

native.country583

target0

dtype: int64

Using the character variables, let us now count the number of values in the data set that are unique.

cat = train.select_dtypes(include=['O'])

cat.apply(pd.Series.nunique)

workclass8

education16

marital.status7

occupation14

relationship6

race5

sex2

native.country41

target2

dtype: int64

Since there are some missing values in all 3 character variables, let's impute these missing values with their respective modes.

#Education

train.workclass.value_counts(sort=True)

train.workclass.fillna('Private',inplace=True)

#Occupation

train.occupation.value_counts(sort=True)

train.occupation.fillna('Prof-specialty',inplace=True)

#Native Country

train['native.country'].value_counts(sort=True)

train['native.country'].fillna('United-States',inplace=True)

We will now need to check if there are any values

missing in the data set.

```
train.isnull().sum()
```

age0

workclass0

fnlwgt0

education0

education.num0

marital.status0

occupation0

relationship0

race0

sex0

capital.gain0

capital.loss0

hours.per.week0

native.country0

target0

dtype: int64

We will now look at the target variable to check if there is any issue within the data set.

#check proportion of target variable

train.target.value_counts()/train.shape[0]

<=50K 0.75919

>50K 0.24081

Name: target, dtype: float64

We can see that seventy-five percent of the variables in this data set belong to the <=50k class, which means that even a rough target prediction will give you a result with a seventy-five percent accuracy. This is amazing, isn't it? Let us now create a cross tab where we will check education using the target variable. This will help us understand if education influences the target variable.

```
pd.crosstab(train.education,
train.target,margins=True)/train.shape[0]
```

target<=50K>50KAll

education

10th0.0267500.0019040.028654

11th0.0342430.0018430.036086

12th0.0122850.0010130.013298

1st-4th0.0049750.0001840.005160

5th-6th0.0097360.0004910.010227

7th-8th0.0186110.0012280.019840

9th0.0149570.0008290.015786

Assoc-acdm0.0246310.0081390.032769

Assoc-voc0.0313570.0110870.042443

Bachelors0.0962500.0682100.164461

Doctorate0.0032860.0093980.012684

HS-grad0.2710600.0514420.322502

Masters0.0234640.0294520.052916

Preschool0.0015660.0000000.001566

Prof-school0.0046990.0129910.017690

Some-college0.1813210.0425970.223918

All0.7591900.2408101.000000

From the above data, we can see that out of the seventy-five percent of the people with a salary above 50k, at least twenty-seven percent of them were high school graduates. This is accurate since people with a lower level of education are not expected to earn more. On the other hand, out of the twenty-five percent of the people with a salary of 50k, five percent of them are high-school graduates while six percent are bachelors. This is a pattern that is of some concern to us, and it is for this reason that we must look at the variables before we come to any conclusion.

Now that you have come this far, you may be

wondering how you should build your very own machine learning model in Python. This is covered in the next chapter. We will, however, look at a little bit of it in the next part of this chapter. For this purpose, we will need to use the scikit learn library, since it will accept numeric data. Therefore, we will need to convert the character variables in the data set into the numeric data type using the labelencoder function. This function will assign every variable a number. For example, let us assume that we have a variable called color, and there are four values in that variable, namely – red, blue, green and yellow. When you use label encoding, you will receive the following data as the output – red = 0, blue = 1, green = 2 and yellow = 4.

#load sklearn and encode all object type variables

from sklearn import preprocessing

for x in train.columns:

if train[x].dtype == 'object':

```
lbl = preprocessing.LabelEncoder()

lbl.fit(list(train[x].values))

train[x] = lbl.transform(list(train[x].values))
```

Let us now look at the changes that we have applied to the data set.

```
train.head()
```

ageworkclassfnlwgteducationeducation.nummari
tal.statusoccupationrelationshipracesexcapital.ga
incapit al.losshours.per.weeknative.countrytarget

0396775169134014121740403 80

150583311913230410013380

23832156461190514100403 80

35332347211725021004038o

4283338409913295200040 40

You will now notice that the variables, including the target variables, have been converted into the numeric data type.

```
#<50K = 0 and >50K = 1
```

```
train.target.value_counts()
```

24720

1 7841

Name: target, dtype: int64 Building a Random Forest Model

Let us check the accuracy of the model by creating a random forest model. from sklearn.model_selection import train_test_split

```
from sklearn.ensemble import
RandomForestClassifier from
sklearn.cross_validation import cross_val_score
from sklearn.metrics import accuracy_score
```

```
y = train['target'] del train['target'] X = train
```

```
X_train,X_test,y_train,y_test                    =
train_test_split(X,y,test_size=0.3,random_state
=1,stratify=y) #train the RF classifier
```

```
clf  =  RandomForestClassifier(n_estimators  =
```

```
500, max_depth = 6) clf.fit(X_train,y_train)

RandomForestClassifier(bootstrap=True,
class_weight=None, criterion='gini',
max_depth=6, max_features='auto',
max_leaf_nodes=None, min_impurity_split=1e-
07, min_samples_leaf=1, min_samples_split=2,
min_weight_fraction_leaf=0.0,
n_estimators=500, n_jobs=1, oob_score=False,
random_state=None, verbose=0,
warm_start=False)

clf.predict(X_test)
```

Let us now check the model's accuracy by making some predictions on the test data set. #make prediction and check model's accuracy

```
prediction = clf.predict(X_test)

acc = accuracy_score(np.array(y_test),prediction)

print ('The accuracy of Random Forest is {}'.format(acc))
```

The accuracy of Random Forest is 0.85198075545.

The learning algorithm has thankfully given us an accuracy of 85%. You can always work around with the program to improve accuracy. In this chapter, we have divided the training data set into two halves and made all our predictions based on that test data set. As an exercise, you should now use this model and make some predictions on the data that we initially loaded into Python. You should follow the steps that we did in the chapter with the new data set to complete your exercise.

Chapter Ten: Building a Machine Learning Model Using SciKit Learn

This chapter will show you how you can build a machine learning model in Python using Scikit-learn. You will need to load the NumPy and SciPy directories to ensure that Scikit learn works correctly, and this must be done before you download Scikit learn. One of the easiest ways to install scikit learn is to use pip.

pip install -U scikit-learn

Let us now begin building the machine learning model.

Step One: Load the Data Set

Every data set will have the following components:

- Features: These are also called the inputs, attributes or predictors, and are the variables or points in the data set. There can be more than one feature in the data set, and it is for this reason that the features are represented in the feature matrix. Feature Names provides the list of the names of every feature.

- Response: A response is also called the label, output or target. The value of this variable is calculated based on the input or feature variable. There will always be a single response variable, and this is represented using the response vector. The target names list contains the values that the response variable can take.

Loading the Example Data Sets[2]

There are some example data sets in scikit-learn, namely the boston house prices data set for regression and iris and digits data set for classification. The data sets can be downloaded from the following locations:

- Boston House Prices: http://archive.ics.uci.edu/ml/datasets/Housing

- Iris: https://en.wikipedia.org/wiki/Iris_flower_data_set

- Digits:http://archive.ics.uci.edu/ml/datasets/Pen-Based+Recognition+of+Handwritten+Digits

---

[2] Archive.ics.uci.edu. (2019). *UCI Machine Learning Repository: Data Set*. [online] Available at: http://archive.ics.uci.edu/ml/datasets/Housing [Accessed 23 Mar. 2019]

The following code will help you understand how to download the example data sets that are present in scikit learn.

load the iris dataset as an example from sklearn.datasets import load_iris iris = load_iris()

store the feature matrix (X) and response vector (y) X = iris.data

y = iris.target

store the feature and target names

feature_names = iris.feature_names

target_names = iris.target_names

printing features and target names of our dataset

print("Feature names:", feature_names)

print("Target names:", target_names)

X and y are numpy arrays print("\nType of X is:", type(X))

printing first 5 input rows print("\nFirst 5 rows of X:\n", X[:5]) The output for the above code is:

Feature names: ['sepal length (cm)','sepal width (cm)', 'petal length (cm)','petal width (cm)']

Target names: ['setosa' 'versicolor' 'virginica'] Type of X is:

First 5 rows of X: [[5.1 3.5 1.4 0.2] [4.9 3. 1.4 0.2] [4.7 3.2 1.3 0.2] [4.6 3.1 1.5 0.2] [5. 3.6 1.4 0.2]]

Loading An External Data Set

You should now consider the case where you will be loading an external data set into scikit learn. We will need to use the pandas library here since this library makes it easier for us to manipulate the data whenever necessary. You can use the following command:

pip install pandas

The following data types are the most important

to know in the Pandas library:

Series: This data type can only hold a one-dimensional labelled array.

DataFrame: A DataFrame is a two-dimensional data structure that is labelled. The columns in this type will use different data types. This is more like an SQL table or a spreadsheet, or a series of objects. This is one of the most used objects in Pandas.

The data set used in the example below is downloaded from the following location:

http://www.sharecsv.com/dl/327fb8f66f90a98c2ed4454665efae9d/weather.csv

```
import pandas as pd

# reading csv file

data = pd.read_csv('weather.csv')

shape of dataset print("Shape:", data.shape)

column names print("\nFeatures:",
```

data.columns)

storing the feature matrix (X) and response vector (y) X = data[data.columns[:-1]]

y = data[data.columns[-1]]

printing first 5 rows of feature matrix

print("\nFeature matrix:\n", X.head())

printing first 5 values of response vector print("\nResponse vector:\n", y.head()) The output for the above code is:

Shape: (14, 5)

Features: Index([u'Outlook', u'Temperature', u'Humidity', u'Windy', u'Play'], dtype='object')

Feature matrix:

Outlook Temperature Humidity Windy 0 overcast hot high False

1 overcast cool normal True

2 overcast mild high True

3 overcast hot normal False

4 rainy mild high False Response vector:

0 yes

1 yes

2 yes

3 yes

4 yes

Name: Play, dtype: object

Step Two: Splitting The Data Set

It is important to determine the accuracy of any machine learning model, and to do this the model must be trained by using a given data set, and the accuracy of the model should be tested using the same data set. The results that the model provides are used to test the model's accuracy. There are many disadvantages of testing the accuracy this way.

- The goal is to maximize the performance of the model with a data set that is not the same as the training data set.

- If you reward the model for predicting the right outcomes using the same training data set, you will develop an overly complex model which cannot be used on other data sets.

- Overly complex models will over-fit the training data.

Therefore, the best option is to divide the data set into two parts – one used for training and the other used for testing the model. In simple words:

- Split the data set into two parts – one the training data set and the other with the testing data set.

- Use the training data set to train the model.

- Now, evaluate the performance of the model using the testing data set.

The advantages of using this method are:

- You can train and test the accuracy of the model using different data sets.

- Since the model only knows the response value for the test data set, you can test the accuracy of the predictions.

Look at the example given below:

load the iris dataset as an example

from sklearn.datasets import load_iris

iris = load_iris()

store the feature matrix (X) and response vector
(y) X = iris.data

y = iris.target

splitting X and y into training and testing sets
from sklearn.model_selection import
train_test_split

X_train, X_test, y_train, y_test =
train_test_split(X, y, test_size=0.4,
random_state=1)

printing the shapes of the new X objects

print(X_train.shape)

print(X_test.shape)

printing the shapes of the new y objects

print(y_train.shape) print(y_test.shape)

The output for the code above is: (90L, 4L)

(60L, 4L) (90L,) (60L,)

The function train_test_split takes many arguments, and these have been explained below:

Variables x and y: These variables represent the features matrix and the response vector. These are the parts that will need to be split.

Test_size: This variable carries the ratio of test data to the data that is given. For example, if the test size is 0.4 for 150 rows, the value of X will be 150*0.4, which is 60 rows.

Random_state: If you use the function random_state = some number, the split will never change. This is a useful command to keep in mind if you want to produce the same results. This will help you test the consistency of the model.

Step Three: Training The Model

We should now train the model using the training data set. You can use different machine learning algorithms that are available in scikit-learn. These algorithms have a consistent or unified interface for predicting accuracy, fitting, etc. In the example below, we are using the K Nearest Neighbours Classifier.

load the iris dataset as an example from sklearn.datasets import load_iris iris = load_iris()

store the feature matrix (X) and response vector (y) X = iris.data

y = iris.target

splitting X and y into training and testing sets from sklearn.model_selection import train_test_split

X_train, X_test, y_train, y_test = train_test_split(X, y, test_size=0.4,

```
    random_state=1)

    # training the model on training set

    from sklearn.neighbors import
    KNeighborsClassifier

    knn = KNeighborsClassifier(n_neighbors=3)

    knn.fit(X_train, y_train)

    making predictions on the testing set y_pred =
    knn.predict(X_test)

    comparing actual response values (y_test) with
    predicted response values (y_pred) from sklearn
    import metrics

    print("kNN model accuracy:",
    metrics.accuracy_score(y_test, y_pred))

    making prediction for out of sample data

    sample = [[3, 5, 4, 2], [2, 3, 5, 4]]

    preds = knn.predict(sample)

    pred_species = [iris.target_names[p] for p in
```

```
preds] print("Predictions:", pred_species)
```

```
# saving the model
```

```
from sklearn.externals import joblib
```

```
joblib.dump(knn, 'iris_knn.pkl')
```

The output of the code above will be:

kNN model accuracy: 0.983333333333

Predictions: ['versicolor', 'virginica']

Chapter Eleven: Building a Neural Network Using Scikit Learn

In this chapter, we will be using the Perceptron class that is in Scikit Learn. We will use this class on the iris data set. Please download this data set from the following location: https://archive.ics.uci.edu/ml/datasets/iris.

```
import numpy as np

from sklearn.datasets import load_iris

from sklearn.linear_model import Perceptron

iris = load_iris()

print(iris.data[:3])

print(iris.data[15:18])

print(iris.data[37:40])
```

we extract only the lengths and widthes of the petals: X = iris.data[:, (2, 3)]

[[5.1 3.5 1.4 0.2] [4.9 3. 1.4 0.2]

[4.7 3.2 1.3 0.2]] [[5.7 4.4 1.5 0.4] [5.4 3.9 1.3 0.4]

[5.1 3.5 1.4 0.3]]

[[4.9 3.1 1.5 0.1]

[4.4 3. 1.3 0.2]

[5.1 3.4 1.5 0.2]]

The labels 0, 1 and 2 are within the iris.label variable. The corresponding species for these labels are:

Iris setosa,

Iris virginica

Iris versicolor

print(iris.target)

[0 0 0 0 0 0 0 0 0 0 0 0 0 0 0 0 0 0 0 0 0 0 0 0

0 0 0 0 0 0 0 0 0 0 0 0 0 0 0 0 0 0 0 0 0 0 0 1

```
1 1 1 1 1 1 1 1 1 1 1 1 1 1 1 1 1 1 1 1 1 1 1 1 1 1 1 1 1 1 1 1 1
1 1 1 1 1 1 1 1 1 1 1 1 1 1 1 1 2 2 2 2 2 2 2 2 2 2 2 2 2 2
2 2 2 2 2 2 2 2 2 2 2 2 2 2 2 2 2 2 2 2 2 2 2 2 2 2 2 2
2 2 2 2 2 2 2 2]
```

We will now combine these classes to create two classes:

Iris setosa

not Iris setosa (this means Iris virginica or Iris versicolor)

```
y = (iris.target==0).astype(np.int8)
print(y)
[1 1 1 1 1 1 1 1 1 1 1 1 1 1 1 1 1 1 1 1 1 1 1 1 1 1 1 1 1 1 1 1 1 1
1 1 1 1 1
1 1 1 1 1 1 1 1 1 1 1 0 0 0 0 0 0 0 0 0 0 0 0 0 0 0 0 0 0 0
0 0 0 0 0 0 0 0 0
0 0 0 0 0 0 0 0 0 0 0 0 0 0 0 0 0 0 0 0 0 0 0 0 0 0 0 0 0 0
0 0 0 0 0 0 0 0 0 0 0 0 0
0 0 0 0 0 0 0 0 0 0 0 0 0 0 0 0 0 0 0 0 0 0 0 0 0 0 0 0 0 0
0 0 0 0 0 0 0 0 0 0 0 0 0
0]
```

The next step is to create a perceptron that will allow you to fix the data for the variables x and y.

```
p = Perceptron(random_state=42,

max_iter=10)

p.fit(X, y)
```

The above code will give you the following output: Perceptron(alpha=0.0001, class_weight=None, eta0=1.0, fit_intercept=True, max_iter=10, n_iter=None, n_jobs=1, penalty=None, random_state=42, shuffle=True, tol=None, verbose=0, warm_start=False) In []:

We are now ready to predict the outputs.

```
values = [[1.5, 0.1], [1.8, 0.4], [1.3,0.2]]

for value in X:

pred = p.predict([value])

print([pred])
```

[array([1], dtype=int8)][3]

Using A Multi-Layer Perceptron

We will now use the multi-layer perceptron (MLP) for this example. This perceptron is an example of a feedforward neural network (explained above). This network will map the input data onto the appropriate outputs. The MLP has many neural layers, and every layer is fully connected to the layer before and after it. The nodes in every layer are neurons and each of these neurons is assigned a non-linear activation function. The nodes or neurons in the input layer do not use this activation function. You can have more than one non-linear hidden layer in the network.

---

[3] Archive.ics.uci.edu. (2019). *UCI Machine Learning Repository: Iris Data Set*. [online] Available at: https://archive.ics.uci.edu/ml/datasets/iris [Accessed 23 Mar. 2019].

Import MLPClassifier from the sklearn.neural_network.

```python
X = [[0., 0.], [0., 1.], [1., 0.], [1., 1.]]

y = [0, 0, 0, 1]

clf = MLPClassifier(solver='lbfgs', alpha=1e-5,

hidden_layer_sizes=(5, 2), random_state=1)

print(clf.fit(X, y))

MLPClassifier(activation='relu', alpha=1e-05,
batch_size='auto', beta_1=0.9,

beta_2=0.999, early_stopping=False,
epsilon=1e-08,

hidden_layer_sizes=(5, 2),
learning_rate='constant',

learning_rate_init=0.001, max_iter=200,
momentum=0.9,

nesterovs_momentum=True, power_t=0.5,
random_state=1, shuffle=True, solver='lbfgs',
tol=0.0001, validation_fraction=0.1,
```

verbose=False, warm_start=False)

The neural network is depicted in the diagram below. This network has been trained for the classifier clf. X_0 and X_1 are the two input nodes in the input layer, and the output neuron or node has been labelled "Out." There are two hidden layers in this network. These layers have the neurons H_{00}, H_{01}, H_{02}, H_{03} and H_{04}. The second hidden layer is made up of the H_{10} and H_{11} neurons. The neurons have a bias in both the hidden and output layers. What we mean by this is that the neuron B_{00} is biased towards the neuron H_{00}, B_{01} is biased towards H_{01} and so on. Every neuron or node that is in the hidden layer will be sent a signal, and the last hidden layer will pass the output to the output layer after adding some weights to the nodes.

$$\sum i=0n-1wixi=w0x0+w1x1+...+wn-1xn-1\sum i=0n-1wixi=w0x0+w1x1+...+wn-1xn-1$$

In the above equation, the value n depicts the number of neurons or nodes present in every layer, wi is used to depict the ith component in the weight vector. You must remember that the hidden layers will need to pass the values to the output layer. This layer will then use a non-linear activation function, $g(\cdot):R\rightarrow Rg(\cdot):R\rightarrow R$, to perform a linear summation. The activation function is a hyperbolic tan function that will now be used on the result.

The attribute coefficient has a list of the weights for every layer in the form of a matrix. The matrix at the index 'i' will show you the weights that are present between the layers 'i' and 'i+1.'

```
print("weights between input and first hidden layer:")

print(clf.coefs_[0])

print("\nweights between first hidden and second hidden layer:")

print(clf.coefs_[1])
```

weights between input and first hidden layer: [[-0.14203691 -1.18304359 -0.85567518 -

4.53250719 -0.60466275] [-0.69781111 -3.5850093 -0.26436018 -4.39161248 0.06644423]] weights between first hidden and second hidden layer: [[0.29179638 -0.14155284]

4.02666592 -0.61556475] [-0.51677234 0.51479708]

7.37215202 -0.31936965]

0.32920668 0.64428109]]

The following is the summation formula that is associated with the Ho neuron:

$\sum i=0n-1wixi=w0x0+w1x1+wB11*B11\sum i=0n-1wix$ $i=w0x0+w1x1+wB11*B11$ This formula can also be written as:

$\sum i=0n-1wixi=w0x0+w1x1+wB11\sum i=0n-1wixi=w$ $0x0+w1x1+wB11$

This is because B11 = 1.

You can use the clf.coefs to obtain the values fo w0 and w1 in the following way: w0=w0= clf.coefs_[0][0][0] and w1=w1= clf.coefs_[0][1][0]

```
print("w0 = ", clf.coefs_[0][0][0]) print("w1 = ", clf.coefs_[0][1][0])
```

```
w0 = -0.14203691267827162
```

```
w1 = -0.6978111149778682
```

You can access the weight vector for H0 by making use of the following code:

```
clf.coefs_[0][:,0]
```

The code above will give you the result:

```
array([-0.14203691, -0.69781111])
```

If you want to create a general line of code to access the different hidden neurons, you can use the code below:

```
for i in range(len(clf.coefs_)):
```

```
number_neurons_in_layer = clf.coefs_[i].shape[1]
```

```
for j in range(number_neurons_in_layer):
```

```
weights = clf.coefs_[i][:,j]
```

```
print(i, j, weights, end=", ")
```

```
print()
```

```
print()
```

```
0 0 [-0.14203691 -0.69781111],
```

```
0 1 [-1.18304359 -3.5850093 ],
```

```
0 2 [-0.85567518 -0.26436018],
```

```
0 3 [-4.53250719 -4.39161248],
```

```
0 4 [-0.60466275 0.06644423],
```

```
1 0 [ 0.29179638 4.02666592 -0.51677234
7.37215202 0.32920668],
```

```
1 1 [-0.14155284 -0.61556475 0.51479708 -
0.31936965 0.64428109],
```

```
2 0 [-4.96774269 -0.86330397],
```

The variable intercepts_ gives you a list of the vectors that have a bias. In this list, the vector in the index 'i' indicates the bias that has been included in the layer 'i+1' by the network.

```
print("The bias values for the hidden layer are:")
```

```
print(clf.intercepts_[0])
```

```
print("\nBias values for second hidden layer:")
```

```
print(clf.intercepts_[1])
```

The bias values for the hidden layer are:

```
[-0.14962269      -0.59232707      -0.5472481
7.02667699 -0.87510813]
```

Bias values for second hidden layer:

```
[-3.61417672 -0.76834882]
```

The objective behind training a classifier is to help the network predict the results for any new sample.

This can be done by making use of the predict method. This method will return a predicted class for any sample.

```
result = clf.predict([[0, 0], [0, 1],

[1, 0], [0, 1],

[1, 1], [2., 2.],

[1.3, 1.3], [2, 4.8]])
```

You do not only have to look at the class results. You can also look at the predict_proba method and derive some probability estimates.

```
prob_results = clf.predict_proba([[0, 0], [0, 1],

[1, 0], [0, 1],
```

[1, 1], [2., 2.],

[1.3, 1.3], [2, 4.8]])

print(prob_results)

[[1.00000000e+000 5.25723951e-101]

[1.00000000e+000 3.71534882e-031]

[1.00000000e+000 6.47069178e-029]

[1.00000000e+000 3.71534882e-031]

[2.07145538e-004 9.99792854e-001]

[2.07145538e-004 9.99792854e-001]

[2.07145538e-004 9.99792854e-001]

[2.07145538e-004 9.99792854e-001]]

Prob_results[i][0] will give you the probability estimate for the zeroth class. [4]

---

[4] Python-course.eu. (2019). *Machine Learning with Python: Neural Networks with Scikit.* [online] Available at: https://www.python-course.eu/neural_networks_with_scikit.php [Accessed 23 Mar. 2019].

Conclusion

Many organizations and businesses use machine learning to improve their processes thereby maximizing their revenue. If you want to do the same for your business, or you simply want to enhance your skills, this book has provided you with the information you need. As mentioned in the book, machine learning and artificial intelligence are two terms that have taken the world by a storm. These terms are not new, but have only become popular over the last decade. This is because people all across the world want to improve their processes.

Since machine learning is a subset of artificial intelligence, many of the concepts that are used in machine learning have been taken from artificial intelligence. It is only when you grasp the concepts of artificial intelligence that you can understand what machine learning is all about. It is important that you know the basics of the subjects that have been mentioned in Chapter one in the book. When you understand the basics of these subjects, like probability and expectations, you can build your very own models on any platform.

You now know that there are different ways in which you can train a machine. You also have some information on the different algorithms that you can use to build a machine learning model. You must, however, remember that there are newer algorithms that have been developed over the years. These algorithms may be complex to understand, and it is for this reason that it would always be a good idea to begin with the algorithms in this book.

You can use different programming languages to do the same. Python, however, is the best option to use. As mentioned in the book, Python is one of the only languages that allows you to use different libraries and packages to build models. Some of the packages you can use have been mentioned in the book, but that is not the exhaustive list. The developers of Python are doing their best to make life easier for people who build machine learning models. They have built many packages and have made them available on Github and on the Python website. It is important for you to learn the basics of Python. Ensure that you understand all the terms used in this book.

This book will help you build your very first machine leaning model and neural network. Before you do this, you need to learn more about how to ensure that the data set can be used by the model. You have covered the different ways in which you can manipulate the data in Python using the NumPy and Pandas libraries. There are other libraries that you can use this for this purpose, and you can use the Internet to gather more information about them. You must remember that the tools used in machine learning are constantly updated and upgraded. Every programmer, a novice or an expert, does his or her best to identify a way to improve a specific machine learning process.

For example, if you look at the code used to build the first neural network, the McCulloch Pitts network, you may not be able to understand it. This is because the code that was available for the developers to use then was not advanced. Now, you have different packages and tools available that make it easier for you to build the network.

Using the examples given in this book, you can build your very own machine learning model or neural network. There are many datasets that are available on the Internet that you can use to build these models. Most data sets that are extracted or pulled from the Internet are not labeled, or there is some issue with the data. There can be missing values, outliers and many other issues. Therefore, you should use the techniques mentioned in this book to clean the data. This will make it easier for you to train the model and test it for its accuracy. You can use the data sets that have been mentioned in the book when you start building a model.

When you are working on a new machine learning model, you can always look for some parts of the code on the Internet. You should remember that someone, somewhere has already thought about the model that you are looking at, and may have already written the code and shared it with the world. You should, therefore, do your best to look for a good source. Use the code that was already written and tweak it for your use. If you want to build the model on your own, you can use the code in the book as the base, and build on that code.

You must remember that there is no end to machine learning. This book will take you through what machine learning is, and help you understand how you can build it in Python. You should, however, try to access more learning material that is available on the Internet and use that material to build your models. There are many developments that are taking place in machine learning, and it is always good to keep yourself abreast with those developments. You should always try to learn more about the other domains that are related to machine learning, including data science and deep learning. This book did shed some light on deep learning, but there is so much more that you should learn about. You can always use machine learning to automate processes at work, especially those processes that predict the future. All you need to do is remember that there is no end to using machine learning in your business.

I hope this book will help you build your machine learning models, and improve the processes that you use. When you master machine learning, you can even build a robot that will run all your processes for you. I hope the information helped you identify ways to automate the processes and tools that you use.

Sources

Learning Model Building in Scikit-learn : A Python Machine Learning Library - GeeksforGeeks. (2019).

Retrieved from

https://www.geeksforgeeks.org/learning-model-building-scikit-learn-python-machine-learning-library/

Building Machine Learning Models in Python with scikit-learn. (2019). Retrieved from https://www.pluralsight.com/courses/python-scikit-learn-building-machine-learning-models

What Is Unsupervised Machine Learning? | DataRobot. (2019). Retrieved from https://www.datarobot.com/wiki/unsupervised-machine-learning/

Reinforcement learning - GeeksforGeeks. (2019). Retrieved from https://www.geeksforgeeks.org/what-is-reinforcement-learning/

An introduction to Reinforcement Learning –
freeCodeCamp.org. (2019). Retrieved from
https://medium.freecodecamp.org/an-
introduction-to-reinforcement-learning-
4339519de419

Machine Learning with Python: Neural Networks
with Scikit. (2019). Retrieved from
https://www.python-
course.eu/neural_networks_with_scikit.php

Introduction To Machine Learning – Towards
Data Science. (2019). Retrieved from
https://towardsdatascience.com/introduction-
to-machine-learning-db7c668822c4

An Introduction to Machine Learning |
DigitalOcean. (2019). Retrieved from
https://www.digitalocean.com/community/tutor
ials/an-introduction-to-machine-learning

9 Applications of Machine Learning from Day-to-
Day Life. (2019). Retrieved from

https://medium.com/app-affairs/9-applications-of-machine-learning-from-day-to-day-life-112a47a 429d0

Team, D. (2019). Top 9 Machine Learning Applications in Real World - DataFlair. Retrieved from https://data-flair.training/blogs/machine-learning-applications/

Team, D. (2019). Advantages and Disadvantages of Machine Learning Language - DataFlair. Retrieved from https://data-flair.training/blogs/advantages-and-disadvantages-of-machine-learning/

Deep learning series 1: Intro to deep learning – Intro to Artificial Intelligence – Medium. (2019).

Retrieved from

https://medium.com/intro-to-artificial-intelligence/deep-learning-series-1-intro-to-deep-learning-abb1780ee20

An Introduction to Deep Learning – Towards Data Science. (2019). Retrieved from https://towardsdatascience.com/an-introduction-to-deep-learning-af63448c122c

Nielsen, M. (2019). Neural Networks and Deep Learning. Retrieved from http://neuralnetworksanddeeplearning.com/chap1.html

A Beginner's Guide to Neural Networks and Deep Learning. (2019). Retrieved from https://skymind.ai/wiki/neural-network

Neural Networks - an overview | ScienceDirect Topics. (2019). Retrieved from https://www.sciencedirect.com/topics/neuroscience/neural-networks

Introduction to Python. (2019). Retrieved from

https://www.w3schools.com/python/python_int
ro.asp

Essential libraries for Machine Learning in
Python – freeCodeCamp.org. (2019). Retrieved
from
https://medium.freecodecamp.org/essential-
libraries-for-machine-learning-in-python-
82a9ada57aeb

Python-course.eu. (2019). *Machine Learning
with Python: Neural Networks with Scikit.*
[online] Available at: https://www.python-
course.eu/neural_networks_with_scikit.php
[Accessed 23 Mar. 2019].

www.ingramcontent.com/pod-product-compliance
Lightning Source LLC
LaVergne TN
LVHW091402190726
843491LV00006B/1222